HUMAN ENGINEERING
Marvel or Menace?

BOOKS BY JOHN LANGONE

Death Is a Noun
A View of the End of Life

Goodbye to Bedlam
Understanding Mental Illness and Retardation

Bombed, Buzzed, Smashed, or . . . Sober
A Book About Alcohol

Human Engineering
Marvel or Menace?

HUMAN ENGINEERING

Marvel or Menace?

JOHN LANGONE

Boston   Little, Brown and Company   Toronto

1/1983
Biol.

FIRST EDITION

T 03/78

Cell diagram on page 33 reprinted with permission of Macmillan Publishing
Co., Inc. from *Principles of Genetics* by Irwin H. Hershowitz. Copyright ©
1973 by Irwin H. Hershowitz.

DNA diagram on page 39 reprinted by permission of John Wiley & Sons, Inc.
from *Textbook of Modern Biology* by Alvin Nason. Copyright © 1965 by
John Wiley & Sons, Inc.

Library of Congress Cataloging in Publication Data

Langone, John, 1929–
    Human engineering, marvel or menace?

    1. Human engineering. I.   Title.
TA166.L28   174'.2   77–26030
ISBN 0–316–51427–6

*Published simultaneously in Canada
by Little, Brown & Company (Canada) Limited*

PRINTED IN THE UNITED STATES OF AMERICA

To my good friend Joy Healey, who has not abandoned his
search for truth, this book is affectionately dedicated

Acknowledgments

In preparing this book, I relied on many sources — medical journals, papers presented at scientific meetings, reference books, newspaper accounts, and interviews that I myself conducted. The sources consulted have been cited whenever possible. I am particularly indebted to my fellow medical and science writers, and to my colleagues in the Kennedy Interfaculty Program in Medical Ethics at Harvard University. While I am grateful to all who helped, I alone am responsible for the book's point of view and any errors it contains.

John Langone
Hingham, Massachusetts
January 1977

Contents

HUMAN ENGINEERING
Marvel or Menace?

1

Introduction

For ages human beings have aspired to be more than what they were created. Improvement, if not perfection, of physical and mental strength has long been considered a desirable goal, and each of us employs different methods to achieve it. Diet and vitamins, exercise and transcendental meditation are among the formulas, each of which offers a do-it-yourself way to fulfill author George Eliot's message, "It is never too late to be what you might have been."

This book, however, is not about any yoga or yogurt path to enlightenment, nor will it tell you where to find the best guru in town. It is, rather, about science's attempts to alter, control, and prolong — indeed, even create — life. It is about changing the very essence of nature, including human nature, through techniques once written about only in science fiction. Among these are all the methods lumped under the phrase "genetic engineering" — transplanting genetic material from one living cell to another, gene surgery, and cloning (which is the manufacture of an exact copy of an individual). It is about altering behavior through drugs and through electrical stimulation and surgery of the brain.

It is also about such phenomena as test-tube babies, and the exciting idea that science may one day find a way for us to grow new limbs and organs, as certain other forms of life can.

Already some of the foregoing ideas are no longer wild speculation but strong possibility; in some cases, what was once possibility is reality. Embryos have been grown in test tubes, artificial viruses and genes have been manufactured, the technique of cloning has been successful with frogs.

However, as scientists take important, though halting, steps toward molding the physical and behavioral characteristics of future generations, and look to the eradication of genetic diseases and deformities, concerns are being voiced over the possible misuse of what has come to be known as human engineering. Many scientists and laypeople are alarmed or uneasy about these new approaches to constructing and reconstructing living matter and mental function. For while the potential benefits are enormous, so too are the risks. Gene copying, for instance, may one day help science to wipe out inherited disease, but it could also be used for more insidious purposes — for instance, an intentional lowering of human intelligence, as envisioned in Aldous Huxley's prophetic book *Brave New World*, which expresses his concern over the dangers of scientific progress.

A number of serious questions are also raised by those fearful of opening a Pandora's box of robotlike humans, of the kind described in George Orwell's *1984*. What kind of humans would we construct if we had the power to change society? Who decides what the mold will be? Suppose a tyrant makes that decision. Would police forces cloned exclusively from the cells of a tough FBI director be the answer to all of our law enforcement problems? What of individuality, that quality that makes you and the rest of the world more interesting? Where would the real "you" be if you were changed by drugs, surgery on your brain, or electricity? Would life be duller with hordes of people exactly like you? Would you really enjoy a tennis match between identical Chris Everts?

Already, legal questions have been raised about the status of children born of artificial insemination. What would be the rights of cloned individuals? Would they be considered illegitimate? There are also social questions. If we were able to wipe out all disease and defect, for example, would we be able to handle the longer life-spans that would result? Would we be prepared to deal with the overloads on food, housing, employment, pension and old-age assistance funds? And what of the dangers involved in accidentally (or deliberately) turning a bacterial Frankenstein's monster loose on the world, a strain against which no antibiotic would work? Or, with indiscriminate probing of the cell's inner workings, what if a new virus were created that might actually cause cancer in humans?

These are some of the questions you should ask as you read through this book, and many more will be suggested. Today they are referred to as bioethical questions, dealing as they do with biology, the science of life, and ethics, the philosophy of human conduct and the determination of right and wrong. Underlying them all is one of the most important, perhaps *the* most important, question: If we are ever able to carry out the sort of bioengineering suggested in this book, should we do it? That question has divided the scientific, religious, and legal communities.

There are extremists on both sides of the issue, as there are in every controversy; there are also advocates of a more moderate course of action. On one end are those who would halt all research involving the manipulation of mind and matter. On the other, those who would proceed at all costs because they believe that all science and knowledge is good, or they believe in science for science's sake alone. Another view, somewhere in between, holds that, while the potential benefits to humankind far outweigh the risks, there must be controls on such research and carefully formulated guidelines.

There are few firm answers to questions involving pure research and ethics, but I hope the reader will feel free at least to form opinions about some of the issues in this book. For better or for worse, the fields of biology and human behavior are growing fast and will undoubtedly alter the course of our lives much more than they already have. It is important that you have as much information as possible about what scientists are doing, and why they are doing it. Only then will you be able to make a judgment about whether or not, or how, they should be pursuing their work. For just as politics is too important to be left to politicians, so is science too important to be left only to scientists.

2
Origins
of Life

In the beginning, according to religion and legend, the creation of life and its habitat was wrought by the hand of God or gods. The Bible's book of Genesis tells us Jehovah created heaven and earth and every living creature that crept, swam, and flew. He formed man from the slime of the earth, woman from one of his ribs. In the Babylonian tale of creation, Marduk, god of light and life, was the creator: "Blood I will form and cause bone to be; then I will set up Lullu, 'Man' shall be his name." The ancient Greeks believed that Athena sprang to life, fully armed, from the head of Zeus; a race of giants from the blood of Uranus. A Borneo legend tells us that a woman who dwelled in the sky, Kinorolungan, created man and woman — out of a termite nest. The Hopi Indians, too, believed that a female, Kokyangwuti, the Spider Woman, fashioned life in the form of twins from earth mixed with her saliva.

Many people today, of course, take the scriptural accounts of creation literally, believing that God carried out His creation in six days, and that He did it directly, that is, without the aid of the slow development process we call evolution. Those who follow this line of reasoning believe that God created Adam, the first man, and "breathed into his face the breath of life, and man became a living soul." While many people still believe that creation of the universe and all that it contains was a supernatural event, such a view is not considered scientific in the strictest of terms, since a divine act is not easily subjected to laboratory analysis.

The "slime of the earth" explanation for life goes back a long way. More than twenty-three hundred years ago, the Greek philosopher Aristotle taught that life originated on earth from nonliving, or inorganic, matter in a process known as spontaneous generation. This notion, also called abiogenesis, had already been widely held for several hundred years, and few questioned the belief — until as late as the early 1800s — that snakes, eels, and frogs arose from marsh mud and damp earth, that tiny white worms were formed by decaying meat, and that insects could be generated in a solution "under electrical influence."

The foundations of this theory were shaken in 1660, however, by the Italian naturalist and poet Francisco Redi, who demonstrated that the maggots that seemed to spring from putrefying meat were actually the eggs of flies. His proof was simple. Redi merely wrapped pieces of meat in fine gauze, thus keeping away the flies and preventing the birth of larvae. What he had done was show that the maggots grew from eggs, that there was no life without prior life.

The evidence that life could not arise from lifeless substance was further strengthened some two hundred years later by the experiments of the French chemist and bacteriologist Louis Pasteur. In a series of classic tests, he showed that the processes of fermentation and putrefaction in beer, wine, and milk were caused by germs. These germs, he said, were not spontaneously generated by the decay processes themselves, nor by some spark of life present in oxygen. Rather, the fermentation came about through contamination from bacteria found in the air to which the various liquids had been exposed. After demonstrating this in a historic lecture at the Sorbonne in Paris in 1864, Pasteur remarked, "Never will the doctrine of spontaneous generation recover from the mortal blow of this simple experiment."

Finally, in 1869 John Tyndall, the Irish physicist, passed a beam of light through the air in a box and showed that whenever dust was present, decay occurred; when it was absent, it did not.

While all of the foregoing does seem to demolish the theory that life arises spontaneously — at least any form of life as we know it today — there is ample reason to believe that at some point early in the earth's history, it did emerge, after a series of steps, from nonliving matter. In a sense, this means that those who believed in abiogenesis were correct in their assumption, which, though simplistic, was not totally out of line with what we know about chemistry today.

There are many scientific theories that attempt to explain how life began on earth. One, known as the panspermia hypothesis, suggests it came to us from outer space, perhaps aboard meteorites. Organic compounds resembling coal, peat, and other products of plant life have, in fact, been detected in meteorites. It is doubtful, however, that living, primitive bacteria could have survived aeons of bombardment by cosmic rays and other radiation that contaminated our early earth. The evidence of life found in these visitors that have sped to us from outer space probably proves only that life is capable of arising somewhere else in our universe, and provides strong evidence for the theory of chemical evolution. But it does not explain how life began, or where it originated.

More probably, life on earth was first formed by chemical action in the primeval atmosphere. The process would have been an excruciatingly slow one, a period of gradual chemical evolution, followed by one of biological evolution, spanning millions of years. (It should be pointed out here that many scientists also hold religious beliefs, and do not deny that the so-called natural laws — those derived from nature or reason — may be of divine origin.)

Some scientists believe that the early universe consisted of a great cloud of a single gas, hydrogen, the simplest of all elements. About thirteen million years ago, there was, according to the theory, an explosion so awesome that it defies description. All the other elements were created in this cataclysmic blast, including some of the key ingredients of life. Thus when the planet earth and the others of our solar system were born some eight billion years later — loosed from the primitive dust cloud that is known as the solar nebula — the raw materials out of which living organisms were destined to arise were already in existence.

In 1936 the Russian biochemist A. I. Oparin theorized that organic compounds, the forerunners of more complex life forms, could have been formed easily from these ingredients. Among these essential components were methane, ammonia, water vapor, and hydrogen, all of which can be converted into amino acids; these, in turn, are the units out of which protein, the chief component of all life, is made. The turbulent primordial environment — a seething chemical "soup," stabbed by lightning, bathed in

radiation from the sun, and blasted by volcanic activity —
provided the necessary energy for the conversion process.

To determine the way life originated, scientists have
attempted to simulate, with a good deal of success, the
primal atmosphere and to create the chemical compounds
necessary for life out of inorganic substances. This was
accomplished in an experiment conducted in 1953 by Dr.
Stanley Miller, then a chemist at the University of Chicago. Miller circulated a mixture of ammonia, methane,
hydrogen, and water past an electrical discharge, and in a
week he did indeed produce amino acids and other molecules that are found in living systems today. Later it was
discovered that ultraviolet light — the invisible rays beyond violet in the solar spectrum — produced similar results. And in 1960 scientists demonstrated that certain
organic chemical compounds could be made from a
watery solution of ammonium cyanide, a compound probably present in the earth's primitive seas.

In another experiment designed to duplicate conditions
in the solar nebula as closely as possible, Dr. Edward
Anders and his colleagues at the University of Chicago
heated carbon monoxide and hydrogen with meteoritic
dust. They obtained a mixture of hydrocarbons, the simplest form of organic matter. The mixture was strikingly
similar to that found in meteorites. This experiment accounted for the hydrocarbons, but the scientists wanted to
find out whether they could produce all the other organic
compounds found in meteorites. To do this, they broad-
ened their experiments, adding other ingredients, such as
ammonia, and varying the heating conditions. At last they
were able to account for nearly all organic compounds
seen in meteorites — among them amino acids and some
of those to be discussed later, such as adenine and guanine.
The last two are key ingredients in DNA, the master

molecule, the chemical carrier of genetic information in our cells.

Dr. Anders's group suggested that a similar process may have given life on earth a head start by contributing to this planet's early supply of organic matter. Meteorites carrying organic material may have fallen on the primitive earth, just as they do today, the larger ones exploding on impact. This could have changed the organic matter to carbon monoxide and hydrogen. Later, when the fireball cooled, the gases could have recombined and produced a fresh supply of organic material, the forerunner of life and even of some of our petroleum supplies.

Remember that no one is absolutely certain that it all began in just this way. But chemists have imitated many of these reactions that take place in nature, and thus it is logical to assume that the chemical events described here did occur as suggested.

Wherever the seeds of life came from — embedded in extraterrestrial meteorites or formed in the poisonous mixture of gases surrounding our planet — at some point in the very distant past they got a toehold in the crust of the earth and in the hot soup of the primal ocean. There is geological proof that this event occurred at least 3.5 billion years ago. Fossil organisms at least that old have been found buried in layers of rock in the Transvaal region of Africa. Among the oldest known microfossils thus far, some are rod-shaped and resemble bacteria, and the others are similar to blue-green algae, a class of water plants that includes seaweed and pond scum.

Somehow the starter materials of life combined in just the right proportions to make the gradual shift from chemical to biological, to form simple, single-celled organisms where there were no cells to begin with. It is believed that these early living organisms were composed of molecules of a substance we've already mentioned, DNA, the chemical combination that dictates inherited traits. Apparently, they were able to duplicate themselves, one of the essential characteristics of a living thing. Sparked by the fierce natural energy swirling about on the new planet, and influenced by the selective pressure of a demanding environment that supported only the hardiest of life forms, these microancestors of ours went on copying themselves. They also were able to mutate, that is, to undergo changes from generation to generation, to enable them to adapt to the harshness of the new world in which they lived.

The ancient atmosphere was empty of oxygen, the colorless, odorless gas that we take for granted, but which is essential to life as we know it. But there are certain organisms that are able to live without oxygen. These are known as anaerobic, and are usually bacteria. Oxygen is actually poisonous to these organisms. Scientists believe anaerobic bacteria were the first life forms on earth.

Later, cells containing chlorophyll (the green coloring matter of plants) began to proliferate in the oceans, and the process of photosynthesis began. Photosynthesis is the formation of carbohydrates (organic compounds important as food to plants and animals) from carbon dioxide and water, through the action of sunlight on chlorophyll. As the chlorophyll cells began to fill the ocean, carbon dioxide — another major component of the earth's early atmosphere — was gradually replaced by the molecular oxygen also being formed in large quantities from water. Many anaerobic cells perished in this toxic environment — toxic to the cells — but others were forced to adapt by developing, scientists believe, a special enzyme called superoxide dismutase. This protected them against the poisonous oxygen.

Throughout the early phases of evolution, these cells joined together in all sorts of combinations. Living and nonliving matter blended again and again, as chemistry meshed with biology, and life forms grew more and more complex. Symbiotic, or mutually beneficial, relationships developed. One theory of symbiosis is that, at some time in the primitive, heaving ocean, a simple bacterium got inside one of the higher forms of cellular life that had emerged. There it lay undigested, somehow helping the cell with the work necessary for it to "breathe," to nourish itself, and to multiply. A larger, single organism developed that may well have been the forerunner of the complicated life forms of today.

Speculations about how life began on earth are important, not only to a better understanding of what transpired on this planet aeons ago, but also to what might be going on right now on other planets in this and other solar systems. The present conditions on Jupiter, for example, are believed to be identical to those of the primitive earth. A rapidly spinning, gigantic ball of gas and liquid, its atmosphere probably contains the same combination of ammonia, methane, hydrogen, and other gases that wrapped itself about the primitive earth. It also has an internal source of heat — 54,000 degrees Fahrenheit — that might be sufficient to trigger some form of life in the distant future. The fierce temperature, scientists believe, is caused by energy left over from the time the planet was created.

While the formation of life may or may not be a chemical law of the universe, one fact is very clear — living organisms *are* capable of adapting to extremely hostile environments, springing up in the most impossible places. Bacteria, for instance, have been found thriving in the radioactive core of nuclear reactors, in corrosive stomach acid, and in strong solutions of sodium hydroxide, a caustic substance used in bleaching and in making soap. Life exists on the ocean floor, in crushing pressures thousands of times stronger than those at sea level, on the edge of the earth's atmosphere, and frozen in glaciers.

Two dramatic examples of life's versatility may be found in environments of opposite harshness — in the steaming hot waters of a bubbling geyser pool in Yellowstone National Park, and in the frigid, Mars-like Dry Valleys of Antarctica at the bottom of the world.

In 1964 Professor Thomas D. Brock, a microbial ecologist at the University of Wisconsin at Madison, equipped himself with a thermometer and a microscope and began a study of Yellowstone's hot springs, where the boiling waters ranged from acid to alkaline, briny to fresh. It had been known for a hundred years that some life was able to live there, but just how extensive it was scientists were unsure. Brock, largely with the support of the National Science Foundation, has gone on studying the geyser basins, and thus far has found that no more than three or four out of the hundreds of springs and basins he has explored are without life. He has identified organisms that thrive at temperatures well beyond the sea-level boiling point of water, and even discovered the first known organism capable of producing a pollutant, sulfuric acid, under high-temperature conditions. He has also established a limit beyond which life seems incapable of maintaining itself — a combination of a temperature close to boiling and an acidity near that of vinegar or lemon juice.

Most of the organisms Brock has investigated are bacteria and algae. Furthermore, he has pointed out, the conditions in the hot springs may be similar to what the earth must have been like several billion years ago, when cellular life first appeared. Yellowstone, Brock has found, is one of the few places in the world in which structures similar to the billion-year-old algal fossils can be seen in the process of formation. However, more advanced forms evolved there as well. Insects, capable of withstanding some of Yellowstone's fierce temperatures, feed on the algae and on each other. There are species of wasp, dragon fly, beetle, mite, and spider; birds like the killdeer feed on those insects and leave their own bodies for the bacteria to return to the energy cycle. Even the few springs that appear to be sterile may turn up some form of life later on, as the scientists refine their microbe-detecting techniques.

Brock has more recently turned his attention to the specialized biochemical substances that enable Yellowstone organisms to survive and adapt to the unfriendly surroundings. There are, for instance, certain enzymes and heredity-related molecules (such as nucleic acid, which will be discussed more fully) that are able to work only at temperatures near the boiling point of water ($212°$ F or $100°$ C) and are ineffective at, for instance, a relatively cool $140°$ F.

Life in Antarctica is another story. The continent is the world's most hostile environment. Buried under 90 percent of the world's ice and snow, some of it two miles deep, it is by far the windiest and coldest place on earth. Temperatures as low as $126.9°$ below zero (F) have been recorded there. No trees or plants grow on Antarctica, and no human being has ever been born there. But penguins, seals, and a variety of fish and bird life have been able to adapt to the bitter cold — along with the few men and women scientists who travel there yearly. Recently bacterial life has been found in areas known as the Dry Valleys, which are among the few ice-free sections of the frozen continent. The valleys are bathed in high ultraviolet radiation, raked by dry winds, and always in the grip of intense cold. The wind-whipped dunes are patterned with cracks like dried pottery. The place is so like Mars that geologic data gathered there have been compared to the photographs returned from the *Viking* Mars mission in 1976. Results of soil studies in the Dry Valleys have convinced scientists that life also can exist on Mars and on other planets. One team of scientists, from Virginia Polytechnic Institute, took several soil samples in which there were no visible microorganisms. Later a single population of bacteria was found in the same area, showing that, with the passage of time and some improvement in the environment, microorganisms could begin to adapt. Even more exciting, though, was the recent find of two scientists from the Darwin Research Institute of Dana Point, California, and the California Institute of Technology's Jet Propulsion Laboratory. Working with a multinational team investigating the continent's evolution, Dr. E. Roy Cameron and Frank A. Morelli, both of whom had also been doing research in the Antarctic under NASA's space program for extraterrestrial life detection on Mars, went to work on several sediment cores drilled out of the permanently frozen ground at various sites in the Valleys. They first passed a butane torch flame over the tubes containing the samples to wipe out any contamination; then, using a sterilized hand drill, they bored into the center of the cores and extracted chips with sterile cotton swabs. Then they took the samples to germ-free laboratories and put them into a nutrient "broth" to see what might grow. It turned out that there were microorganisms in the cores, that they had been there for anywhere between ten thousand and a million years, and, more startling, they revived, grew, and reproduced. Only one type refused to grow, although it lived. "We could all see them wiggling when we observed them under the microscope," said Dr. Cameron, "but conditions were apparently not right for them to grow." One type formed unusual doughnut-shaped colonies that grew or flowed in toward the center as the colony expanded; then, according to Dr. Cameron, they collectively took on the shape of an inactive volcano. None of the bacteria has yet been identified, although all were motile — that is, equipped with fine, hairlike appendages that propel them. The results of the core experiments, Dr. Cameron feels, could have tremendous relevance to understanding the ability of microorganisms to remain frozen in a state of suspended animation for hundreds of thousands of years. Furthermore, he believes, scientists attempting to detect life on Mars might well speculate, on the basis of the Dry Valley borings, that even if no life forms are found on the surface of the planet, the subsurface permafrost may well hold the key to ancient and living organisms buried deep within it, which thrived at some distant time when the Martian atmosphere was more hospitable to life than it appears to be now.

Recently, three other scientists at the California Institute of Technology discovered that fossil shells of an extinct mollusk, a hard-shelled invertebrate animal, were so well preserved even after eighty million years of burial that they still contained proteins. It was the first time intact proteins had been found in such ancient fossils. Ordinarily, when a living organism dies, its proteins decompose rapidly and are either washed away or consumed by other organisms.

Life, then, or its various components, can show up virtually anywhere — here, or on one of the untold planets circling stars, with energy sources able to touch off the biochemical reactions that make life possible. Astronomers, in fact, have speculated that 5 percent of the myriad stars in the universe have around them the same suitable conditions that our sun has, and that have helped create life on this planet. This amounts to millions of opportunities for the existence of life in some form or other.

Furthermore, unless the laws that govern chemistry, physics, and biology differ from solar system to solar system, there does appear to be a common thread running through all living things. We will look a bit later at this bond that is present in the smallest bacterium to the largest elephant. Suffice it to say for the moment that recent discoveries in biochemistry have shown that what we know as life results from a complicated arrangement of only a few chemical units, and that this unique interaction must have gone on long before we were the specialized creatures that we are now. As Dr. Cyril Ponnamperuma, a professor of chemistry at the University of Maryland, put it at a recent meeting of the American Association for the Advancement of Science: "The idea of the biological unity of everything living, and the evolution of the higher forms of life from the lower — an idea which caused a revolt among the humanists of the nineteenth century — is today the cornerstone of modern biology. If this concept is pushed to its logical conclusion, another form of evolution has to be postulated, prior to biological evolution, namely, chemical evolution."

Scientists, as we will see later, have been able to string the few basic chemical units together in just the right way to create, in a test tube, identical copies of natural genes, the bearers of heredity. They have, in effect, cracked the code of life, successfully planting these artificial genes in bacteria and watching them work, as well as those "born" in the microorganism. Just how far science will be able to go in this synthesis of life processes, or in the manipulation of genes, remains to be seen. Again, Dr. Ponnamperuma has said: "There is no reason to doubt that we shall rediscover, one by one, the physical and chemical conditions which once determined and directed the intermediate steps in the laboratory. Looking back upon the biochemical understanding gained during the span of one human generation, we have the right to be quite optimistic. In contrast to unconscious nature which had to spend billions of years, conscious nature has a purpose and knows the outcome. After all, what we need to do is to produce the smallest living entity."

3

Genetics and the Spiral Staircase

Next time you look into a mirror, gaze into your eyes, those remarkable, colorful organs of sight whose worth and beauty have been sung in story and song. Each is an intricate camera with a lens that focuses colored pictures on a sensitive film. The film is the retina, located at the back of the eye, and after the pictures are registered there, they are sent along the optic nerve to the brain. But just how they are transmitted, and how they are actually seen by us, remains unclear.

Equally baffling is how these sophisticated organs arose and developed at all. Geneticists, specialists in that branch of biology that deals with inheritance, assume that the eyes emerged gradually in the same slow mutational process that changed single-celled organisms to simple, multicellular forms, and then directed these, in turn, so that some evolved into plants, others into insects, and still others into animals. Some organs, like the appendix in humans, became small and useless, while others, like the eye, developed new and improved characteristics and powers that enabled them to survive in more complex form.

All of the diverse forms that life on earth takes — there are probably close to two million species of known living organisms — might give one the impression that they were the product of some joke played by a thoroughly unorganized Mother Nature. Actually, there is profound order in the entire process. For our purposes, it does not matter whether it all began with or without the hand of God in it, whether it was planned or merely the result of a dice toss. What is important is that life was probably the result of just the right combination of chemicals and conditions — a combination that does not exist on earth at the present time, but which might exist, right now, on other planets in our solar system.

Not everyone, of course, agrees that life was ordered by the laws of chemistry, biology, and physics. Some scientists believe that life is a unique occurrence, a historical event that could have *not* happened just as easily as it did happen; and that the phenomenon we know as a human being only *seems* special to us because of the powers of its highly developed brain — not because it is the result of a particular plan.

Also essential to any discussion of life and genetics is the fact that all life on this earth — be it microbe or mosquito, a stand of wheat or a newborn baby — not only has the ability to reproduce itself but is made up of cells. And these cells all contain genes, the units responsible for inheritance — with each gene made up of the same wondrous chemical. This chemical is DNA, short for deoxyribonucleic acid.

But let's back up for a moment, about one hundred years, to the time of an Austrian monk, Gregor Johann

Mendel. Before DNA was known, and indeed before the structure of the cell itself was mapped, Mendel first demonstrated experimentally the phenomenon we know as genetic inheritance. This is the mechanism through which various characteristics are passed along from one generation to another. The work for which Mendel is best known involved common garden peas, but it applies to everything that lives. What the monk did was grow many generations of pea plants, using the seeds of each generation. Beginning with purebred plants — that is, those grown from a recognized strain and not mixed with any others — he observed that their seeds always produced plants with similar traits, one generation after the other. Seeds from red-flowered, purebred pea plants, for instance, invariably brought forth red-flowered plants.

Next Mendel began to hybridize his plants — crossbreeding, or mixing, dwarf varieties; he mixed dwarfed plants with tall ones, red-flowered plants with white-flowered ones, and so on. He did this by transferring the pollen — the tiny reproductive cells of flowering plants — from one variety to another. As each of his hybrids ripened, he collected the seeds from their pods and replanted them, spring after spring. Careful observation turned up a number of important facts. One was that the results of the cross-breeding were not what might be expected. That is, mixing the pollen of a red-flowered plant with that of a white one did not produce a reddish-white flower. Nor did a plant of average height result from the union of a short and a tall one. What did happen, Mendel discovered, was that each new plant inherited certain traits as complete units, and that these units (now known to be genes) were passed along in pure form to subsequent generations. Thus, cross-breeding tall plants with short ones produced plants that were either tall or short — with the plants of the first generation all more likely to be tall. Likewise, the first-generation plants that resulted from a cross between red and white produced only red plants.

However, Mendel discovered also that when he cross-bred first-generation hybrids with each other, the result could be white-flowering plants or dwarfs. This meant that the ingredients for short and tall, and for red and white, were ever present and could show up at any time in future generations. These hereditary units, Mendel learned, occur in pairs, one from the mother and one from the father for each trait. One of these genes may predominate over the other — in a human being, this might mean that you inherit your mother's brown eyes rather than your father's blue ones. In a pea plant, a particular gene is responsible for the red flower over the white one, or the tall plant instead of the short one. The stronger gene is termed dominant, the other, recessive. However, even though you may have inherited your mother's blue eyes, the recessive gene for brown eyes is very much a part of your genetic makeup and may show up in your children or in theirs. Remember also that chance plays a large part in determining which genes you receive, and there is a broad range of ways an offspring can turn out.

Mendel's work, like that of many other men and women who were far ahead of their time, was not fully appreciated until several years after his death. In 1900 scientists digging through the dry literature of biology rediscovered the quiet monk's experimental data in the pages of an obscure journal. Later other scientists confirmed Mendel's findings, not only in plants but in animals. The science of genetics with its laws of heredity had burst on the scene, and scientists were now better able to understand the answer to what had been a puzzling question: What makes each individual different from every other?

Genetics is the study of variation, of differences that are passed along, and of all the biochemical elements in our cells that make each of us unique. It is a complex science, but there is a precise order to it all, particularly in the way the chemicals in our bodies combine to produce a particular fingernail or a hair, a bit of skin or a drop of blood, and in how these chemicals mix to influence our emotions. All of it is directed from within the genes, miniature storehouses of information that lie packed inside the threadlike chromosomes, found in the nuclei of all living cells — whether they be in a hawk's eye or a fly's egg.

Of course, genetics is not entirely responsible for our individuality, nor for any abnormality that we may have. It is very difficult to separate the role of heredity from the role of environment in the development of the individual. The English scientist Sir Francis Galton (1822–1911) referred to the two factors in human development as nature and nurture. The first, nature, means the genes that we inherit from our parents; nurture refers to all of the social and physical circumstances of our daily lives. Nurture includes such factors as: being rich, poor, or middle-class; our nutritional and working habits; even the effects of our exposure to viruses and environmental pollutants.

There is little doubt that environment is crucial to what we become. Just how crucial, no one can really say — at least insofar as humans are concerned. In pea plants and frogs, it is relatively easy to separate out the genetic factors simply by cross-breeding, as Mendel did, and to manipulate the environment to suit the experiment. One might, for example, deliberately withhold nourishment from a mouse to determine the effects of such a drastic move on it or its offspring. But for studying human beings, these experiments are not possible — or at least not advisable. About the only course left open to a geneticist is to manipulate and mate cells in a test tube, and to observe closely all of the peculiarities and similarities that crop up in families, and in individual members of a wide variety of populations.

A cousin of the famed naturalist Charles Darwin, whose explorations and observations led to a classic concept of evolution, Galton was the founder of the science of eugenics. This is the technique of improving a race or breed by selectively mating individuals with desired characteristics. Galton believed strongly that if society really wishes to excel, then it must cultivate only the worthwhile talents, and stifle the negative traits, such as poor health and weak intelligence. Successful individuals, he suggested, should have more children than should lesser people. His best-known work dealt with the inheritance of talent of all kinds — artistic, scholarly, and athletic. (A system of fingerprint identification he developed also won him prominence.) Playing down the role of the social environment, Galton gathered an enormous amount of data from records of prominent families to support his theories of inheritance. "Nurturists" disapproved of his findings, claiming that a favorable environment, not inheritance, was the dominating influence in the lives of the children of talented and successful parents.

Nazi dictator Adolf Hitler's horrifying attempt at eugenics stands as a chilling example of misplaced values and abuse of power, as well as a misinterpretation and exaggeration of what eugenics means. In the fall of 1939, Hitler signed an order calling for the extermination of all people who were mentally defective or who had incurable disease. By December of that year, several thousand unfortunates had been led off to execution camps to be shot. Compulsory death for the useless and the undesirable,

Hitler reasoned, not only would improve the species but would conserve food and free necessary hospital beds. The eugenics program was classified top secret, and friends and relatives of the executed were told only that they had died of some illness. Though the program was halted in 1941, more than 275,000 persons, many of them Germans, perished. Hitler also used the gas chamber to murder millions of Jews, a people he saw as unfit to live.

In a classic account of how such a dictatorship can turn medical science into a horror, Boston psychiatrist Leo Alexander has told of how a German specialist in nerve disease received some five hundred brains from the killing centers for the insane. Dr. Alexander, who served as consultant to the U.S. secretary of war during the famous war-crimes trials of Nazis at Nuremberg, quotes the German scientist as saying: "There was wonderful material among those brains, beautiful mental defectives, malformations and early infantile diseases. I accepted those brains, of course; where they came from and how they came to me was really none of my business."

In addition to the "material" the German doctor wanted, several other cases were mixed in — patients with Parkinson's disease, depression, brain tumors, and severe mental illness. "These were selected from the various wards of the institutions according to an excessively simple and quick method," said the doctor. "Most institutions did not have enough physicians, and what physicians there were were either too busy or did not care, and they delegated the selection to the nurses and attendants. Whoever looked sick or was otherwise a problem was put on a list and was transported to the killing center. The worst thing about this business was that it produced a certain brutalization of the nursing personnel. They got to simply picking out those whom they did not like and the doctors had so many patients that they did not even know them, and put their names on the list."

Galton, of course, did not advocate anything like this. The battle, however, between nature and nurture still goes on, and scientists still cannot say for certain which, if either, is more important in the area of special talents. Was the Austrian composer Mozart, for example, brilliant in his field because his father was a celebrated concert-master, violinist, and author? Many children grow up in a similar artistic environment but do not demonstrate the same talents of mother or father. Geneticists see examples like Mozart as proof that unusual talent is inherited. As Dr. H. J. Muller, a Nobel laureate from Indiana University, has suggested: "An individual is rarely outstanding in a particular ability or predisposition unless not only his environment but also his heredity was markedly inclined in that direction."

Few would argue that poverty, despair, and lack of education have some effect on the mind, can stunt intellectual growth, or even lead a person into a life of crime. But geneticists know too that a host of abnormalities, physical and emotional, can be traced to inherited defects in the cells, defects that are linked to some imbalance in the body's chemical makeup.

Consider schizophrenia, humankind's most widespread mental crippler. A severe emotional disorder, the most important symptom of which is withdrawal from reality, schizophrenia has long been associated with family environment — if not caused by it, certainly strengthened by frightening and domineering treatment, even neglect, of a child during his or her growing years. Today, however, more and more attention is being paid to the suggestion that the disease is a physical one, just as arthritis and diabetes are physical diseases. In fact, many researchers now believe that an error in the body's chemistry, perhaps inherited, is at the heart of the problem. We know, of course, that many diseases are inherited, passed on through the genes from parent to offspring. One of these is the blood disorder hemophilia, which is transmitted by females, who are not generally affected by it, to male offspring. Some people also inherit a tendency toward a certain disease, as opposed to actually inheriting the disorder itself. Such people begin life with some built-in weakness that makes them prone to disease. For instance, you don't inherit an allergy like hay fever. You may, however, be born with a predisposition, a tendency, to become allergic. If both your parents are allergic, or if there is allergy on both sides of your family, chances are that you, your brothers and sisters will develop an allergy.

After Mendel's studies were rediscovered and publicized, the American scientist Thomas Hunt Morgan (1866–1945) began experimenting with a lowly creature, the rapidly multiplying fruit fly called *Drosophila melanogaster*. Morgan (who later was to receive a Nobel Prize, in recognition of his work in establishing that genes line themselves up on the cell's chromosomes) did what Mendel did, substituting the tiny flies for pea plants. In 1910, working in a laboratory that came to be known as the "fly room" at Columbia University, Morgan noticed a small variation in a male fly buzzing about in one of his bottles. The fly had white eye color instead of the normal red color. The scientist bred the fly with its red-eyed sisters to find out what would happen. All of the offspring had red eyes. Further matings among the generation produced a second generation, some of which had white eyes. All of them, however, were males. Still further matings showed that the white eyes almost always turned up in males; but, once in a while, a white-eyed female would also appear. Morgan thus was able to demonstrate that red was predominant over white — a typical example of what has come to be known as a Mendelian factor. Morgan referred to the white-eyed condition as sex-limited (later changed to sex-linked), meaning that the genes for white eyes were located on the female chromosome in each individual, the so-called X chromosome. Sex is determined by two chromosomes, X and Y. Normally the female complement is XX, the male XY. Morgan's work showed for the first time that hereditary characteristics are linked to a specific chromosome. It is important to remember too that the X chromosome bears not only genes related to sex but also genes for such disorders as color blindness and hemophilia. These traits are among the ones inherited by the mechanism of sex-linkage.

Which brings us back to the cell, that smallest basic unit of life, and all that it contains. It is a busy place, and highly organized. Bacteria are made up of only one cell; the human body consists of trillions, of different shapes and having different purposes. Red blood cells carry oxygen and carbon dioxide; nerve cells carry messages to and from the brain. Some cells are rod-shaped, some star-shaped; others are shaped like saucers, or rectangles, or they are shapeless blobs. There are cells in a maple leaf and in an ant's leg, in sponges beneath the sea, and in the skin of an embryo nestled in its mother's womb. Some cells, like the single-celled amoeba, are loners, free-living creatures that move formlessly and without any apparent purpose through the soil, or the water, or as parasites in animals. Others are specialists, each with a job description spelled out in its genes. Such cells are part of the structure of higher organisms. They band together in "communities" where each performs its special task, forming organs and tissues that make up an entire creature.

The English physicist Robert Hooke (1635–1703), a mechanical genius who anticipated some of the most important discoveries and inventions of his time, was the first person to use the term "cell." His noted work *Micrographia* referred to the structure he saw in plants through his crude microscope as "little boxes or cells, distinct from one another." But it was not until 1838 that the cell was recognized as the basic structural unit of all plant life. For this we can credit the German botanist Matthias Jacob Schleiden (1804–1881), who saw that vegetable tissues develop from and are constructed of groups of cells, with the nucleus playing the most significant part in each cell. A short time later, another German scientist, Theodor Schwann, determined that not only plants but animals too are composed of cells. "There is one universal principle of development for the elementary parts of organisms, however different," said Schwann, "and that principle is the formation of cells."

Though the rude, low-power microscopes of these early scientists revealed only the hazy outlines of the cell, and an even hazier view of what lay inside, the groundwork had been prepared, and there was not much doubt that the cell was the elemental unit of biological organization and function.

But it was not until the invention of the electron microscope in the 1930s that biologists were able to get a near-perfect look at the cell's shadowy interior. There is no upward limit to magnification with a standard optical, or light, microscope. But there is a limit to useful magnification, and this is determined by what is called resolving power. This means the capacity of the microscope to

bring fine detail into focus. High magnification with limited resolving power — some modern light microscopes
can magnify up to two thousand times — only makes the
object larger and fuzzier. The electron microscope, which
is over a hundred times as powerful as the strongest
light microscope, has revealed the complexity of cellular
organization with remarkable clarity. Instead of light rays
and lenses, it works with electrons — minute atomic particles that revolve around the nucleus of the atom and
carry a negative electric charge — and electromagnetic
fields. In essence, the electron microscope beams a stream
of electrons — which also make up the current that lights
a light bulb — through a thin slice of the material to be
examined. It magnifies the shadow created by denser
parts of the sample, making the shadow visible on a
screen, something like that of a television set. It also
records the shadow on film. The first electron micrograph
of a cell was made in 1945, and although its quality as a
photograph was poor compared to modern standards, it
was nonetheless a significant achievement.

Thus magnified, the once-shrouded inner workings of
the cell are revealed, and though a good deal is still too
small even for the electron microscope, what we are now
able to see almost stuns the imagination. For inside the
thin, pulsing, porous membrane, which wraps the cell like
a sausage casing, is a teeming microworld, full of the stuff
of life itself. It is a gelatinous place of perpetual motion,
where each of the cell's many components floats about like
wreckage on a heaving sea. Indeed each living human cell
is a miniature sea, containing all of the salts found in the
oceans of earth, doubtless our inheritance from the days
when one of our fishlike ancestors mutated, becoming a
reptile that crawled up onto the still-steaming land.

Our analogy to an ocean ends there, however. For al-

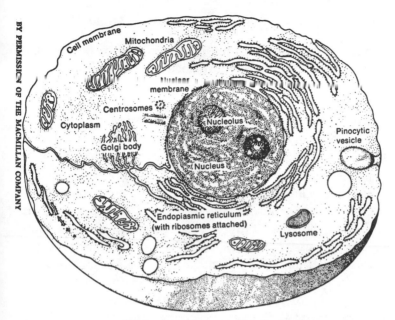

Structure of a generalized cell

though the cell's tiny bits and pieces appear to be drifting aimlessly, like so much flotsam, they actually are functioning in perfect harmony to carry out the cell's main work, which is the manufacture and use of vital proteins of all kinds, for itself and for other cells.

Proteins are the familiar muscle-builders found in meat, fish, milk, cheese, eggs, and beans. As we grow, our bodies gain new cells, and proteins are essential for growth. They also help repair damaged or worn-out cells. Without protein our bodies would not make enough cells to maintain good health.

But proteins are much more than simple body-builders. They are extremely complicated molecules, or combinations of atoms, made up of the amino acids. They often combine with other substances, such as carbohydrates, fats, and nucleic acid. The latter is a biochemical agent that includes the master chemical DNA.

Since a molecule of protein is made up of hundreds or thousands of amino-acid molecules, depending on the molecule, the different arrangements are countless. There are accordingly many different kinds of protein, thousands, in fact. Some are responsible for the actual structure of the cell's walls, and of such tissues as skin and hair. Others, called enzymes, speed up the thousands of changes that take place regularly in our bodies. There are more than one hundred thousand of these chemical workhorses in every human cell. Without enzyme action, you would not be able to digest your food, replace your blood cells, build tissue, or even take a breath. Whenever a gene wants something done, it makes a specific enzyme to do the job. And, turned the other way around, when something goes wrong with a gene, something also happens to the enzyme that it is supposed to produce, and disease may result. When this happens, the defective enzyme function — inherited as a sex-linked characteristic — is usually traced to a specific site on the X chromosome.

There are proteins called hormones, chemical regulators carried by the blood from the endocrine glands to other parts of the body, where they stimulate some physical reaction, and can even affect our emotions. The hormone adrenaline, for example, floods the bloodstream in times of stress and drives up blood pressure. The heart beats faster, the pupils of the eyes expand, the muscles tense, and stomach juices are inhibited, thus impairing digestion. All because of a particular protein.

Despite the wide variety of proteins, they have one important thing in common: each one is manufactured in the miniature chemical laboratory of the cell, according to an exact set of instructions sent out by the carrier of genetic information, DNA.

The story of DNA and its role in heredity is probably

the most important and exciting scientific story of this century, and some understanding of how the chemical works and what it does is essential to any discussion of genetics and genetic engineering. It is also an involved tale, almost as tangled as the way DNA actually appears under an electron microscope.

The story begins in 1868, in the laboratory of a Swiss biochemist, Johan Friedrich Miescher. Miescher had been studying the cell nucleus, the round control center that contains, among other elements, the chromosomes. He had been trying to break down, with a digestive enzyme, the protein that he suspected cells were made of. But, although he was able to do this to the cell, he found that his enzyme didn't work the same way on the nucleus. Struck by its refusal to break up, Miescher analyzed it and saw that it contained large quantities of a strange substance that was very unlike protein. He called it nuclein. And although Miescher had no idea of its importance, he had discovered what came to be known years later as nucleic acid, the chemical family to which DNA belongs.

In 1944 a team of scientists from the Rockefeller Institute — Oswald T. Avery, Colin M. MacLeod, and Maclyn McCarty — demonstrated for the first time that DNA was the bearer of hereditary information. They did this by extracting some of it in pure form from a bacterium, and using it to replace a defective gene in another related bacterium.

Nearly ten years later, James D. Watson, a young Harvard biochemist, and physicist Francis Crick of Great Britain, finally described the intricate molecular structure of DNA. This turned out to be a double helix, or twisted ladder, a spiral staircase that is capable of unhinging itself as it brings about the two most important activities in a cell's life. One of these is reproducing itself exactly by dividing in two, a process known as mitosis. The other is manufacturing protein. DNA, scientists now realized, was the biological "missing link" between living and nonliving matter. Soon after, they also broke the genetic code that DNA employs to order the manufacture of protein.

Exactly how does a cell's machinery "read" the genetic instructions in DNA, and use them to produce exact replicas of itself again and again and again? Just what is this code, this formula for life? How is it used to make protein?

Let's back up a moment, to the chromosomes in the cell's nucleus. A human being is conceived when a female egg, one of thousands that develop in a woman's ovaries, is fertilized by a single one of several hundred million sperm that each male produces in his testes. At this moment of fertilization the child's sex is determined, as well as his or her hereditary traits. The fertilized egg, called a zygote, now carries forty-six chromosomes — twenty-three from the mother and twenty-three from the father — if the process goes normally. These microscopic strands of chromosomes occur in pairs, and each living thing, plant or animal, has a distinctive, predetermined number. White rats, for instance, have forty-two; pea plants have fourteen; corn, twenty; Drosophila, the fruit fly, eight; and the tiny rhizopod, a one-celled creature, an incredible fifteen hundred. Human beings, as we have said, always have forty-six unless something goes awry, as in the genetic disorder called Down's syndrome, also known as mongolism. Children afflicted with the disorder are mentally retarded. They also carry, for some unexplained reason, an extra chromosome, for a total of forty-seven.

If we examine a chromosome closely, we see that it is

sectioned into genes that are made up of very long, slender molecules of two-stranded DNA, twisted together and wound around an inner core of protein. Every human cell has twenty-three pairs of DNA strands, corresponding with the number of chromosomes from each of two parents. If we could stretch out a single cell's DNA molecules, they would reach for several feet, many thousands of times the width of the cell itself. It would be well to pause here for a moment and reflect on the incredibly tiny world with which we are dealing.

A woman's ovum, for example, is one of the largest cells in the body. This egg cell measures about 130 microns, or one two-hundredth of an inch, in diameter; this makes it just about visible to the naked eye. Average body cells are about 30 microns across, which means that a thousand of them laid end to end would measure about an inch. But consider the long-tailed sperm cell, whose head measures only 5 microns long. Science writer Amram Scheinfeld has put this infinitesimal world into perspective this way: "How fantastically minute the genes are becomes apparent if you think, first, of the microscopic size of a sperm — its whole length being only ½₅th that of a comma on this page. Then recall that the head of a sperm, only about one-twelfth its total length, contains 23 chromosomes. And now consider that these chromosomes may contain, collectively, about 30,000 genes (with hundreds, or a thousand or more of them in any one chromosome) and that *a single gene*, in some cases, may be able to change the whole life of an individual!"

After a female ovum is fertilized by a sperm and endowed with all the traits spelled out in the genes — eye color, body build, and sex, to name a few — it begins to drift down the ducts that connect the ovaries to the womb. As it floats slowly along, it begins to divide in two, then into four, eight, sixteen, and many more cells. About a week after conception, the cell mass, about one-fiftieth of an inch in diameter, attaches itself to the soft wall of the uterus, or womb. There it undergoes further doublings, arranging and rearranging itself, while the cells change their shape and function, mate with other cells, and then find a place to settle. In time, there are billions of cells; next come the development of skin, organs, nervous system, and skeleton, until a whole human body has been formed. Sometimes something goes wrong with the way the cell behaves. It may, for instance, grow uncontrollably when it should be slowing down and settling into a routine. The result may be cancer.

So often is a baby born that we hardly think twice about the process. And if anyone asks us how it has happened, we may be able to offer a vague explanation about sperm and egg uniting, growing into an embryo, and then into a fetus that is finally expelled from the womb after about nine months. But there is so much more to it than that. If we agree that the process of conception and birth is impressive, even miraculous, then we must be absolutely awed by what occurs at the microscopic level of the gene, which is in the chromosome, which is in the head of the sperm and in the nucleus of every other living cell, be it in a colorful chrysanthemum, a drab-looking cockroach, or a heavyweight boxer. And the best place from which to watch this drama of life unfold is the spiral staircase where it all takes place. A word of caution before we begin. The following passages are not meant to be an exact description of what happens in a living cell, or in a test tube where scientists duplicate some of the steps outlined. Remember that these are *chemical* reactions, and any seeming similarity to a Tinker Toy being assembled, snapped apart, and assembled again — imagined by either the reader or the author — is purely for the sake of description.

The double helix, we have said, is made up of twisted strands of DNA. There are more than ten billion miles of it in the total number of cells in an adult human body, yet it is so compact that all of it would fit easily into a pillbox.

First, let's take a close look at the twisted chemical ladder itself. A chemist would find no unfamiliar substances among its various parts, which are called nucleotides. The spiral sides of the ladder are phosphates, which are combinations of the mineral phosphorus and oxygen, and sugars. The rungs are made of four chemical molecules — adenine, guanine, cystosine, and thymine (A, G, C, and T). Each rung actually consists of two of the chemicals, joined in the middle. For example, a half-rung of C always joins with a half-rung of G to form a whole rung; an A

Structure of the DNA molecule

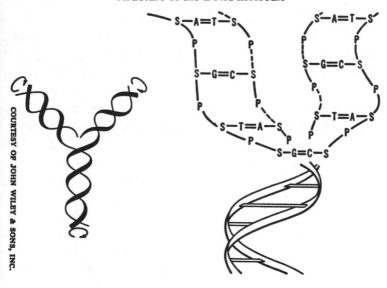

always ties into a T. But the rungs can ascend (or descend, depending on how we look at the ladder), and the possible arrangements of the steps are almost endless. For instance, a set of steps, or rungs, might look like this: CG, GC, AT, TA, TA, AT, CG, CG, GC, GC, AT, GC, AT, and so on. A virus might contain some two hundred thousand DNA rungs arranged in different sequences. A germ might have five or six million rungs in its chromosomes. A single human cell, the top of the line of life, contains mind-boggling billions. But whatever the form of life — man, mouse, or microbe — it is all composed of the same chemical ladder. It is the *order* in which this four-letter chemical alphabet is arranged that "spells" out what form life will take, and gives each gene its own special code to direct the manufacture of the protein for which it is responsible.

Consider, in the simplest possible terms, how the cell uses that alphabet to write out the unique combination of matter we know as life. Remember, though, that this molecular language is so detailed that the amount of information contained in the DNA of only one cell would fill many volumes of reference books. One thing, however, makes the language a little less cryptic. That is that every one of the thousands of genes in a cell has a specific niche in a chromosome, and a special function to perform. The gene that codes for your hair color, for instance, is always in its own place on the "program." When you consider the thousands of different proteins that go into a human body — each the handiwork of only one gene — you begin to get some idea of how busy a chemical factory a cell is.

The action begins when the DNA ladder unwinds and the rungs pull apart in the middle, a process that occurs every time a cell begins its ritual of dividing. All of the Cs unhook from the Gs, the Ts from the As. But soon each freed side of the ladder with its half-rungs picks up new nucleotides that are always floating about in the cell. The Cs, Gs, Ts, and As on the ladder halves link up with their proper floating partners, and new ladder sides are formed. Now, where there was one twisted ladder there are two, identical in every way. Each new cell has its own DNA ladder in a new set of chromosomes, and each ladder comes fully equipped with the same coded genetic instructions that its parent has, because its rungs are arranged in the same precise sequence. So, each time a cell duplicates itself, so does its DNA.

The next step is for the cell to use the instructions coded in the genes. It does so in a manner somewhat like an architect passing blueprints to a construction engineer. The blueprints, in this case the genes, contain the coded instructions for making a specific protein. What happens is this: a section of DNA, a gene, "unzips" itself again and makes another nucleic acid, called messenger RNA, or mRNA. In doing so, the gene hands over to the messenger the entire coded blueprint for one protein. This done, it zips itself up once more. The messenger now moves out of the nucleus into the cell's cytoplasm, carrying the instructions to one of the dense granules, called ribosomes, that lie scattered about. These are, in effect, the workshops where the proteins are assembled. At a ribosome, messenger RNA acts like a computer tape, running out its coded message, which contains a "grocery list" of every amino acid needed to make the designated protein. The code is made up of groups of three-letter chemical "words," or triplets, each triplet standing for an amino acid: for example, GGC, ACU, or GUU. (The U stands for uracil, which replaces the T, thymine, in RNA.)

Another form of RNA now enters the picture. Called transfer RNA, or tRNA, it takes the instructions and floats out into the cytoplasm to hunt down the amino acids called for in the triplet code. After linking up with the right amino acid, the transfer RNA takes it to the ribosome where, with the help of messenger RNA, a protein with a special function is assembled.

Interestingly, while there are only twenty different protein amino acids, they can be sequenced in myriad ways to build all of the proteins required for a human being.

Next occurs one of cell biology's least-understood events, the process called cell differentiation. Recall that after an egg is fertilized by a sperm, it divides many times until it is a mass of cells attached to the wall of the mother's uterus. As it matures there, somehow, and at some predetermined time, all of the cells in the mass that will eventually become a male or a female begin to take on a special role, duplicating at different rates and behaving in various ways. One becomes a brain cell, another an eye cell, a bone cell, a liver cell, or a skin cell. Though why this all happens is not fully understood, scientists believe it has something to do with what they call the activator-repressor mechanism. In effect, this is a "switch" that turns certain genes on and off, governing the production of distinctive organs, such as liver, heart, or brain, or when and where necessary nutrients are to be used up. The control system is also what prevents an eye from growing from a fingertip. Without this control, such a mistake could happen, because the genes that code for eye structure are also present in the hand. In fact, every single cell contains the full set of blueprints for the whole life form it represents. It is difficult to imagine — but nonetheless true — that a tiny cell in your fingertip is packed with all the DNA information required to construct another you, as closely similar as a Xerox copy is to the original typescript.

The genes are all there. But each cell expresses itself in a different way, that is, it uses its information specifically. Cells, then, are not said to be differentiated because they contain different information from one another — it is simply a matter of how each one uses the identical information it shares with the rest. Remember that if the on-off mechanism malfunctions, birth defects and cancer may show up.

A single error in the genetic code — a "word" misspelled or a "paragraph" misplaced — can induce a complicated disease involving many organs. Important chemicals may not be made if the production line breaks down or malfunctions, or they could accumulate in dangerous amounts, clogging the body's brain and arteries. A coding mistake in DNA can also lead to its making the wrong kind of protein. Scientists have suggested that errors in the genetic code may in some cases have to do with the aging process. Genetic material might become faulty with age and lose its memory, as it were. The result is flawed protein and bodily slowdown. Several researchers lean toward the idea that DNA degeneration may be due to errors piled up during the repetitive copying process. All of the raveling and unraveling increases the risk of damage to the copying mechanism, until finally the cell's damage-control machinery is unable to deal with the cumulative accidents. If DNA becomes an inaccurate blueprint, then trouble is sure to result.

In chromosomal abnormalities, such as Down's syndrome, more genes than nature intended may be present, or some may be missing, producing multiple inherited defects. The disease called phenylketonuria, or PKU for short, is an example of a gene gone amiss, which, in turn, adversely affects its specific enzyme workhorse. PKU begins at birth, affecting one in 14,300. It nearly always results in mental retardation, unless the individual is placed on a special diet during the early years of life. Scientists now know that PKU produces a genetic enzyme defect, which means an inability to convert an essential amino acid into another essential building block. This amino acid breaks down and begins interfering with brain development. In another such disease, galactosemia, an enzyme defect prevents the body from using sugar properly. Untreated cases result in retardation, malnutrition, even death. Tay-Sachs disease, which occurs chiefly among Jewish children and is usually fatal in the early years of life, is another inherited disorder. Marked by lack of coordination because the nervous system deteriorates rapidly, Tay-Sachs disease is caused by an accumulation of fatty substances in the brain cells, which, in turn, is caused by the lack of an enzyme that under normal conditions directs the breakdown of fatty substances and other cell products.

There is also a chromosomal abnormality known as the XYY syndrome. Some scientists feel it is linked to emotional disturbance and criminal behavior. Sex, as noted earlier, is determined by two chromosomes, X and Y. They are so designated because they actually look like tiny Xs and Ys under a microscope. Normally, the male is XY, the female XX. But in one of every five hundred male births, the complement is XXY rather than XY, with the error leaning toward femaleness. The error in the opposite direction is called XYY, resulting in what is sometimes referred to as "supermaleness." Individuals with this abnormal complement of genes are unusually tall, somewhat retarded, and may be more aggressive than normal males because of the extra bit of chemical information they carry. Several studies, however, have discredited the notion that the extra Y chromosome makes vicious supermen who commit crimes of violence because of a message in their genes. Rather, these studies suggest that, while these men have a higher rate of criminal convictions than normal males do, it may be due to their lower intelligence.

There is a danger in putting too much store in an XYY diagnosis. If, for instance, chromosome studies done at birth turn up an XYY child, he could well be discriminated against all of his life, even though he might never become a criminal.

In any event, there are at least twenty-five inherited metabolic diseases that can lead to mental retardation. Often abnormalities can be detected during the fetal stage. Ultrasonic diagnostic devices are now used to scan pregnant women for birth defects in the fetus, much as a sonar device in a ship uses a sound pulse to locate an invisible enemy submarine. Identification of defects is also possible through a technique known as amniocentesis, undergone by thousands of pregnant women a year. This involves drawing off small amounts of the amniotic fluid that surrounds the infant in its mother's womb. The cells it contains are from the fetus's skin and the sac it has been floating in, and these are studied to determine fetal health or genetic damage. Fetologists, as the specialists who deal with the fetus are called, learn many valuable clues from the cells — fetal age and sex, and any present chromosomal abnormalities, illnesses due to poisons absorbed from organisms in the system, maternal diabetes, or Rh disease, a blood disorder. Dozens of hereditary diseases have been successfully treated and controlled because of amniocentesis.

Fetology may eventually enable surgeons to operate on malformed and diseased fetuses long before they are born — and it may also bring scientists the knowledge they need to allow them to manipulate and rearrange genes to correct birth defects, even at the earliest stage of development.

For all these reasons, scientists have been looking for ways to repress the appearance of injurious gene products and, on the other hand, to stimulate underactive genes. By doing these things they may someday be able to right a chemical wrong. At the moment, about all a physician can do is advise certain couples not to have children because of the possibility of genetic damage. Or, as happens in so many cases when a serious genetic defect is turned up by amniocentesis, the doctor may only be able to offer the remedy of an abortion. Many people have no qualms about abortion when a prenatal diagnosis reveals that the fetus undoubtedly will be severely retarded or otherwise handicapped. Others, however, are opposed to the procedure on moral and religious grounds. If fetal defects could be repaired at an early stage, it would make matters easier for couples who are torn between the probability of having a deformed child and their own deep conviction that the fetus is a human person, the deliberate destruction of whom is murder.

4

Test-Tube Babies

Aldous Huxley's satirical novel *Brave New World*, with its blend of science and literature, painted a grim picture of the year 632 A.F. ("After Ford," automaker Henry Ford, that is). Its theme, as Huxley himself described it, was not the advancement of science as such, but the advancement of science as it affects individuals. In the book, human embryos, all alike, are developed in bottles in the Central London Hatchery and conditioned to be passive. Electric shock treatment is administered to produce the desired effect.

The following passage describes a scene in which some bottled embryos pass through a tunnel:

"Heat conditioning," said Mr. Foster.

Hot tunnels alternated with cool tunnels. Coolness was wedded to discomfort in the form of hard x-rays. By the time they were decanted (born) the embryos had a horror of cold. They were predestined to emigrate to the tropics to be miners and acetate silk spinners and steel workers. Later on, their minds would be made to endorse the judgment of their bodies.

"We condition them to thrive on heat," concluded Mr. Foster. "Our colleagues upstairs will teach them to love it."

And this:

On Rack 10, rows of next generation's chemical workers were being trained in toleration of lead, caustic soda, tar, chlorine. The first of a batch of two hundred and fifty embryonic rocket-plane engineers was just passing the eleven hundred metre mark on Rack 3. A special mechanism kept their containers in constant rotation.

"To improve their sense of balance," Mr. Foster explained. "Doing repairs on the outside of a rocket in mid-air is a ticklish job."

Huxley's baby factories have not yet come to pass, but there is little doubt, given the current pace of scientific research in embryology, that a human fetus will someday be conceived outside the body of its mother, and then grown and nurtured under totally artificial conditions. The techniques for producing a genuine "test-tube baby" are well known, and it is merely a matter of learning a little more about what happens during reproduction, and what chemical conditions must be present for sperm and egg to unite successfully outside the body. The last step would be to fashion an appropriate artificial womb, complete with amniotic fluid, to simulate the natural one. We may also see the day when cloning, a nonsexual method of reproduction aimed at producing children genetically identical to their parents, will be commonplace.

References to the creation of an embryo without benefit of a mother's womb go back much farther than Huxley. Consider for a moment a fascinating individual from the sixteenth century, a Swiss alchemist with a name as flamboyant as the man — Aureolus Philippus Theophrastus Bombastus von Hohenheim. He is better known by the name he assumed, Paracelsus, which implied he was greater than a renowned physician and writer named Celsus. Paracelsus and the rest of the alchemists of the era employed all manner of strange "decoctions," "quintessences," and "electuaries" in their never-ending quest for the philosopher's stone, a mysterious substance they believed would enable them to convert all base metals into gold. They toiled in steaming, foul-smelling laboratories, and most of them eventually claimed to have discovered the stone, or something like it. Part of their quest was also for a universal cure for old age and even death.

Whatever their shortcomings, the alchemists did lay the foundation of modern chemistry, and Paracelsus himself introduced numerous medicines and drugs, among them opium. Insisting that medicine was a branch of chemistry, Paracelsus taught that to restore a person to good health it was first necessary to see that the body's chemicals were in proper balance.

His ideas about embryology are rather interesting, particularly when viewed against modern laboratory attempts to create life. Paracelsus talked of a "homunculus," a tiny human being that could be produced, at least according to the alchemist's fancies, without a natural father. He wrote:

The *generatio homunculi* has until now been kept very secret, and so very little was publickly known about it that the old philosophers have doubted its possibility. But I know that such things may be accomplished by spagyric art assisted by natural processes. If the sperm, enclosed in a hermetically sealed glass, is buried in horse manure for about 40 days, and properly magnetized, it may begin to live and move. After such a time it bears the form and resemblance of a human being, but it will be transparent and without a corpus. If it is now artificially fed with the *arcanum sanguinis hominis* [secret blood of man] until it is about 40 weeks old, and if allowed to remain during that time in the horse manure in a continually equal temperature, it will grow into a human child with all its members developed like any other child such as may have been born by a woman. Only, it will be smaller. We call such a being a homunculus, and it may be raised and educated like any other child until it is grown older and obtains reason and intellect and is able to take care of itself.

As bizarre as such a theory may appear, it did not reach the fanciful heights achieved by an unnamed Tyrolean count in 1775, who supposedly made ten homunculi — a king, a queen, a knight, a monk, a nun, an architect, a miner, a high-ranking angel, a blue spirit, and a red spirit — with the help of an Italian mystic. Kept in water-filled bottles, these miniature humans swam about and eventually grew so large, according to the tale, that they burst from their glass prisons and escaped into the world.

Paracelsus and other alchemists who claimed to have generated life were reproached for their beliefs and experiments, but surely their ideas were no more outlandish than a good deal of what has been translated into modern laboratory research.

Oral contraceptives, for example, have been developed to prevent a woman from discharging an egg cell from her ovaries. These synthetic hormones permit sexual intercourse without pregnancy. There is also donor artificial insemination, a technique known to animal breeders for centuries; it is used when producing a prize line of cattle and horses. In fact, artificial insemination, often referred to erroneously as the production of test-tube babies, has been used to conceive human beings since the late 1800s, and there are thousands of individuals who were born in this manner.

With human beings, as with various animals, the female egg is fertilized when the male's penis is inserted into the the woman's vagina during sexual intercourse, and hundreds of millions of sperm are discharged. This is known as insemination. But if the husband is infertile, that is, his sperm are either inactive or in short supply, the egg cell will not be fertilized and therefore conception cannot occur. In cases such as this, couples who wish to have children may decide on artificial insemination. This is done by taking sperm — which has been drawn from an anonymous donor and frozen — thawing it out, and depositing it in the female reproductive tract during the height of the woman's fertile period. The donated sperm, which may live while frozen in sperm banks for as long as ten years, perform exactly as they would during ejaculation (the male's sudden ejection of semen, or reproductive fluid that carries the sperm, during intercourse). The egg is fertilized, and pregnancy results.

Donor artificial insemination poses several problems. For one thing, long-term storage of sperm — in vats of liquid nitrogen kept at 321 degrees below zero — may cause it to lose its potency or alter its genetic message. A few years ago, the Council on Population of the American Public Health Association said that, although there have been reports of healthy children born from sperm frozen for ten years, these do not mean that such sperm will always produce offspring. The council issued its statement because many men who plan to undergo a sterilization operation, or vasectomy, decide that it might be a good idea to have some sperm frozen for use at a later date, and may be led to believe by some commercial sperm banks that their "seed" is good indefinitely. One physician who has expressed a reservation about commercial sperm-banking is Dr. W. Paul Dmowski, head of the fertility clinic at Chicago's Michael Reese Hospital. He does not believe that all men are capable of having their sperm frozen and stored. "It has been found that some men with normal reproductive potential produce sperm that does not survive freezing," he has observed. "As yet, there is no adequate explanation for this, but there is a great variation in survival among different specimens."

With some men, according to a report in *American Medical News* (1976), only 5 percent of sperm in a given sample survive freezing and thawing. At the extreme end, 70 percent survive, the highest survival percentage attained in Dr. Dmowski's clinic. The clinic's donors, incidentally, are paid for their sperm. They are married men of prime reproductive age who have at least one child. Before their sperm is donated, their medical histories are carefully taken, and they are given laboratory tests and a physical examination to screen for hereditary disease and drug use.

Another troublesome point about artificial insemination is that, as with every other form of human engineering, there is the possibility for its misuse. If, for instance, only sperm from certain "prize" donors were accepted, a master race might be created over time, if only because people have biases and preferences about races and personality traits. We can, of course, predict to some extent what a child will look like and whether he or she is likely to be born with a defect. But we don't really know in exactly which generation the blue eyes or the dwarf plant will turn up, or which offspring will be most intelligent or have the best disposition. The code language of life has an enormously extensive "vocabulary" of chemical and environmental factors, and while scientists are able to converse in it more expertly than in years past, they still are unable to give us a tailor-made individual. The cloth might be the same, but the cut of the clothing, the style, takes some doing.

What science may achieve soon, though, is increasing the odds of a boy or a girl being born; this could be done through sperm-screening and sperm-treatment techniques. Recent research has, in fact, brought us a step closer to the day when a couple might be able to pick the sex of their child before it is conceived. Scientists have already done this in amimals. In recent experiments at Memorial Sloan-Kettering Cancer Center in New York, and at Cornell University Medical College, researchers were able to artificially alter the normal male-to-female ratio of offspring in laboratory mice. They found that natural test litters yielded a 53 percent proportion of males (a slight excess of male births is the norm among mammals), but that artificial insemination, using sperm previously treated with a special serum, produced litters that were 45 percent male. Reporting in the British journal *Nature*, Dr. Edward A. Boyse, an immunologist at Sloan-Kettering Institute, and Dr. Dorothea Bennett, professor of anatomy at Cornell, explained that the serum contained antibodies hostile to a compound found on the surface of all male cells. Antibodies are proteins in blood serum that are formed in response to specific foreign proteins, or disease-causing antigens. They are the body's disease-fighters, our natural defense against the invading antigens. The antibody-antigen reaction is at work when our tissues are filled with bacteria that have streamed in through a cut or wound. The body immediately mobilizes teams of specialized cells and sends them to the wound. Some of these cells wrap themselves around the invaders, recognize them as hostile, and sap them of strength with digestive enzymes. The antibody-containing serum used by the Sloan-Kettering researchers — called an antiserum — had the effect of immunizing the females against the male factor. Even though the experiment increased the production of female births by only 8 percent, it was significant and, as the journal pointed out in a related editorial, could have considerable economic importance in the breeding of farm livestock. A farm might, for instance, breed more dairy cows, thus increasing the production of milk, butter, and cheese. If a method could be found to influence the sex ratio to favor males, more bull calves might be produced, and thus more beef cattle.

What the Sloan-Kettering-Cornell researchers did was use their antiserum to selectively eliminate sperm bearing the male, or Y, chromosome. Another group at the Schering Laboratories in Berlin the same year developed a technique to screen out female-producing X chromosomes from sperm, using the sperm left over for artificial insemination. Recall that the sex of all mammalian offspring is determined by the egg being fertilized by sperm containing either an X (female) or a Y (male) chromosome. X-bearing sperm and Y-bearing sperm are made in roughly equal numbers, with the egg itself always containing one X. A female has no Y. A male, however, can produce sperm with either an X or a Y, which means that male and female offspring will be more or less equally produced. The German experiment was based on the slow "swimming" ability of the X-bearing sperm. (All sperm, incidentally, move by the whiplash action of a tail, or flagellum.) This is probably due to the fact that the X chromosome contains more DNA and is thus heavier than the Y. By letting sperm swim through a thick solution, the scientists found out that the Y-bearing ones got through, but the weaker-swimming Xs did not. With this method, it might someday be possible to collect Y sperm and increase the percentage of male offspring, even among human beings, through artificial insemination. In the Berlin experiment, the scientists were able to raise the percentage of Y sperm from 50 to 85 percent.

Another application of sperm separation might be the development of a filter — one that a woman could use during intercourse — to screen out undesirable or defective sperm. Such a method is a long way from reality, but it is not too far from the grasp of biological research.

A method of reproduction that could sweep in on some future wave is known as *in vitro* fertilization. (*In vitro* is Latin for "in glass," or in the test tube. *In vivo*, another term used in biology, means "in the living body," or in the living organism.) This method entails removing an egg cell from an animal's ovary, fertilizing it in a laboratory culture dish, and allowing it to divide and redivide, until it reaches the stage where it can attach itself to the inside wall of the womb. This point, known as the blastocyst stage, occurs when there is a cluster of about sixteen cells in place of the original one. The blastocyst, or blastula, is then returned to the womb of the donor, or another female, where it implants itself and grows into a fetus. Successful laboratory fertilizations have been achieved for some years, and the technique has enabled many animals — rats, mice, rabbits, and cats — to give birth to live young.

A method similar to *in vitro* fertilization is embryo transfer. This means transferring a fertilized egg from one animal to another. The foster mother then carries the fetus to term. Already the method has been used successfully in pigs, baboons, cows, and sheep. In 1973 a calf was grown in this fashion from an embryo that had been removed from its mother and frozen for a week before it was implanted in another cow. The calf, a Hereford bull born at an agricultural research station near Cambridge, England, was the first large animal ever to be developed from a frozen embryo. In that case, scientists said it would be generations before they could tell whether the deep freeze and subsequent transfer would result in genetic damage or changes. The calf, however, had a natural birth and was in good health.

Two years later, the first nonhuman primate infant, a baboon, was produced by embryo transfer at the Southwest Foundation for Research and Education in San Antonio, Texas. A male, it weighed 30.6 ounces at birth and appeared entirely normal.

The technique has great potential for breeding livestock, such as cattle and horses. For example, fertilized eggs could be frozen and stored long after the death of the parents, and then transported, to be used when needed. Better productivity might also result. Recently researchers at the University of California reported that seven sets of twin calves were born from eggs fertilized outside the cow, then surgically implanted inside the mother. Since cows normally have twins only about 3 percent of the time, the achievement was good news for cattle breeders.

If more twin calves could be produced, the beef industry would benefit, and prices we pay for the meat could be lower.

Embryo transfer is important for different reasons when it involves primates. Apes and monkeys possess certain genetic characteristics that make them particularly worthwhile models for the study of diseases involving humans — who are, after all, members of the same family. One example of possible future applications of embryo transfer is the production of specific strains of nonhuman primates for biomedical research on such human ailments as diabetes, heart disease, and cancer.

But what about using techniques like *in vitro* fertilization and embryo transfer to produce human beings? Will it ever be done? The answer is, I believe, unquestionably yes. As far as is known, no human embryo has been carried to term after the egg cell was fertilized outside the body, or within the body and then transferred elsewhere. A few years ago there were reports from Great Britain that three test-tube babies had been born in Europe and were living normal lives. Nothing, however, has been published in the scientific literature to substantiate these claims.

Nevertheless a number of interesting developments that stop just short of the birth of a test-tube baby have been recorded, developments that make it virtually certain that soon *in vitro* fertilization will produce a full-grown baby, perhaps even as you read this.

One of the first scientists to claim test-tube fertilization of a human egg cell was Dr. Daniele Petrucci, a physiologist at the University of Bologna, Italy. Dr. Petrucci added that his fertilized egg grew to the embryo stage, complete with heartbeat. He said he destroyed the embryo because it was malformed, and he apparently took no photographs of the embryo nor published his results in a research journal.

Other research on human *in vitro* fertilization, however, has been published and widely reported. In 1969 a team in Great Britain, led by Dr. Robert Edwards of Cambridge University, began fertilizing human eggs in the laboratory, mixing sperm and eggs in glass dishes kept at just the right temperature. The scientists held off implanting any of the eggs in a living womb, however, apparently fearful that tinkering with an artificially fertilized egg might alter the DNA in its chromosomes enough to cause birth defects. One of the main reasons for performing such research is that it might benefit women whose Fallopian tubes (which conduct the egg from ovary to uterus) are blocked, a situation that renders a female sterile because the sperm find it difficult to meet the egg under such circumstances. Sometimes, too, pregnancy can develop inside one of the tubes. This is called an ectopic pregnancy, a term that means pregnancy "out of the normal place." If the tube ruptures, an internal hemorrhage may result, and only surgery can save the mother's life.

In 1973 a group of doctors at Queen Victoria Hospital in Melbourne, Australia, succeeded for the first time in fertilizing an egg cell in a test tube, and then implanting it in a thirty-six-year-old woman who had a blocked Fallopian tube and had had the other removed in an operation. The team, including Drs. John Leeton and Carl Wood, first removed sperm from the woman's husband and combined it, in a test tube, with an egg, or ovum, drawn from the woman's remaining ovary. The ovum, taken from the ovary four hours before insemination, was kept alive in its own natural fluid in an atmosphere of 90 percent nitrogen and 10 percent carbon dioxide. About a day after insemination, the egg's outer layer disappeared, an indication of normal growth. The egg was then transferred into a special growth solution containing serum taken from cows, and kept at a temperature of ninety-nine degrees. After forty-three hours, the egg had divided into three cells, and by sixty-seven hours had reached the eight-cell division stage. At seventy-four hours after fertilization, the egg was placed in a plastic tube and inserted into the mother's womb, while the doctors monitored its every movement with a special microscope. Finally, on the fourth and fifth days after the egg was implanted, there were definite indications that the embryo was developing. Proof of pregnancy was further obtained by the female's excretion of a growth-stimulating hormone. While the procedure was a technical success, the fetus survived for only nine days before it aborted. The reason may have been a surgical problem from another operation performed on the woman only a few days before the implantation.

More recently, in 1976, Dr. R. G. Edwards of Cambridge University and his colleague, Dr. Patrick C. Steptoe, revealed in the British medical journal *Lancet* that they too had reimplanted a laboratory-fertilized embryo in a thirty-five-year-old woman. Unfortunately, the fetus was an ectopic pregnancy and had to be removed after thirteen weeks of growth.

Although neither of these experiments resulted in a full-term baby, they are proof that test-tube fertilization is not only possible, but may well be the answer for some of the 2.5 million childless couples in the United States, who may desire children but cannot have them because the women have blocked oviducts. Commented Dr. Leeton in an interview with *Medical Tribune:* "The work we've been doing is clinically oriented. We saw a need for women with blocked tubes to have this done so they could have children. We can't see any problems in this area. It's morally acceptable. But in the long term — and I don't think this will happen in my lifetime — I can see big problems arising."

Dr. Leeton said also that he believed the era is not far off when it will be possible to fertilize one woman's ovum in a test tube, and then implant it in another woman's womb. This, he said, could lead to a new occupation for women — that of an "incubator" for other women's children. For instance, a woman who did not wish to leave her job might hire a human "incubator" to bear her child.

Up till now, we have been talking about *sexual* reproduction of animals and human beings, the way sperm and egg from different sexes fuse to eventually form a mature offspring. But nature knows several other ways that do not require participation of both sexes. For example, the single-celled amoeba and some multicellular animals, such as sponges and jellyfish, reproduce *asexually*, that is, from only one parent. In the case of the sea creatures, as the cells divide they form growths, or "buds," on the body of the parent. These outgrowths later separate to become new individuals, identical to the parent. This process should not be confused with what biologists know as hermaphroditism, which is a variation of normal sexual reproduction. One earthworm, for example, is capable of producing both sperm and eggs. It can therefore fertilize its own eggs to produce another individual.

A form of sexual reproduction occurring in some organisms that normally reproduce sexually is called parthenogenesis. It is also known as "virgin birth." Parthenogenesis involves the development of offspring even though the egg is unfertilized. The best-known example is the bee; it produces queens and workers from its fertilized eggs, and stingless male drones that gather no honey from its unfertilized eggs. These virgin births sometimes occur in turkeys, and they have been induced by chemical or mechanical stimulation in laboratory experiments with several animals.

Scientists in fact have long known that a number of stimuli — high and low temperatures, light, vigorous shaking or stirring, and nutrients — can force a cell to divide. Botanists have thus prodded plant cells to replicate again and again until they become full-grown plants; even a whole carrot was grown in this way in an experiment some years ago.

By simply poking a hole in a frog's egg, scientists can also initiate cell division and subsequent growth to tadpole and then frog — all without benefit of male sperm. Unfertilized rabbit eggs, too, have been goaded into reproducing by being cooled at just the right moment of development. And it is now entirely possible to create a whole fatherless rabbit from such an egg.

Theoretically experiments like these should be successful in other mammals, including women who, for one reason or another, might desire a child without a father's involvement. Carrying this prospect to an extreme, one could imagine being faced with groups of strongly militant feminists crying only for "Mother Power." In our own time, several vocal lesbians have already insisted that parthenogenesis is the answer for colleagues who may want children but who wish to avoid sexual contact with males.

All of which leads us to cloning, an asexual method of producing an exact copy of the parent by transplanting desirable DNA from one cell to an egg. One might think of identical twins as clones. About a third as common as fraternal twins — those that develop from two eggs fertilized by separate sperm — identical twins come from one egg fertilized by one sperm. They are always of the same sex, and have exactly the same hair and eye color. They are, in effect, carbon copies of one another. But they are, of course, the result of sexual reproduction.

Cloning has already produced a laboratory frog. In a 1968 experiment that signaled what biology may have in store for the human race, Dr. John B. Gurdon of Oxford University removed an unfertilized egg cell from a frog and destroyed its DNA-containing nucleus with radiation. He was able to do this without injuring the rest of the egg cell. Next, using a delicate microsurgical technique, he managed to remove the nucleus from a cell in a tadpole's intestinal tissue. He transplanted it into the egg cell with the missing nucleus and watched in amazement as the egg, which now had been given a complete set of chromosomes instead of the half amount found in an unfertilized egg, divided and eventually formed a complete tadpole — exactly like the one that owned the transplanted nucleus.

The experiment proved that the nucleus of every living cell, no matter where in the body it is found, contains the full set of blueprints from which an identical copy of the parent can be made. Even if Dr. Gurdon had used a nucleus from another part of the tadpole, from a skin cell, for instance, the result would have been the same — a carbon copy of the entire original donor.

While human cloning has not yet been accomplished because, for one thing, enormous technical difficulties still remain, the frog experiments of Dr. Gurdon and others have set the stage. Presumably one could remove an egg cell from a woman and destroy the nucleus, replacing it with one from, for instance, the skin cell of a physically powerful and brilliant man. The previously unfertilized egg cell would now act the same as a fertilized one. What is more, it would be loaded with selected DNA. After careful nurturing in the laboratory and after the proper number of divisions, the genetically engineered cell would thon bo implanted in the womb that was to bear the cloned individual.

Apart from the technical obstacles that need to be overcome — a human egg cell, for one thing, is much tinier than a frog's, and the microsurgical instruments necessary to remove and transplant nuclei have not yet been fully developed — human cloning isn't done also because it may not be in the best interests of society to manufacture hordes of selected, genetically identical people. Most biologists, in fact, appear to want no part of cloning beyond the satisfaction of their scientific curiosity about whether it can be done.

A number of serious questions are raised by each and every one of the techniques outlined in this chapter, and we should consider them carefully, every time the science of genetics is discussed. This is not to say, of course, that we must ignore the multitude of potential benefits to be derived from such research and the other work that will be examined in the pages ahead — such benefits as enabling a childless couple to have a child they can love, the cure and prevention of the more than two thousand human genetic diseases by deleting "bad" genes, meeting world food needs by producing more plentiful and hardier livestock, and even duplicating species of wildlife that are endangered.

But artificial insemination, test-tube babies, and cloning should and do give us pause. We have already mentioned that frozen sperm as is used in donor artificial insemination could sustain genetic damage if kept in a deep freeze for long periods of time. The same difficulty may be present when egg and sperm are mingled outside the mother's womb, in a laboratory dish. No one really knows for sure what adverse effects this artificial environment might have on a fragile, dividing cell — particularly if the crucial temperature at which it must be maintained is accidentally altered even a degree or two; or if some sudden jolt in the laboratory shakes the culture dish, nudging the delicate cellular contents into a harmful collision that might result, after implantation, in the birth of a handicapped or deformed human being. And there might be, as pointed out earlier, the danger that a tyrannical race of supermen could be created, for example, or, just as bad, tribes of slaves.

Within the last few years, many scientists and ethicists have raised these issues and others to back up their demands for a moratorium on further efforts to produce a test-tube baby or a clone. Implantation of artifically fertilized eggs, they believe, is unethical experimentation on possible future human beings. Moreover, they question whether it should be medicine's goal to enable women to bear children by any means that might be hazardous to the woman or to the child, even before it is conceived.

One of the most respected ethicists to warn of the dangers of moving too close to Huxley's *Brave New World* is Dr. Paul Ramsey, professor of religion at Princeton University, and a member of the Advisory Council on Medical Ethics of the Judicial Council of the American Medical Association. "Artificial fertilization followed by implantation is an immoral experiment on a possible future human life unless the possibility of damage can be definitely excluded," Dr. Ramsey wrote in the AMA's journal in 1972. "Since this condition cannot be met, at least not by the first 'successful' cases, any man's or woman's venture to begin human life in this way is morally forbidden." Dr. Ramsey also cited two typical arguments in favor of continuing such research, and responded to each. One argument goes like this: The possible future human being could have certain advantages, despite the possibility of induced damage due to artificial production, because intensive scanning could discover early and eliminate natural inborn "errors." Dr. Ramsey refuted this argument, saying that the alleged compensating advantage — the avoidance of a life of pain and suffering from inborn natural errors — is no real advantage to the artificially induced fetus. This is so because the fetus would not have been subject to those very risks had it not been artificially conceived in the first place. A second argument is that artificial fertilization and implantation is only a "therapy" for curing a woman's infertility. Dr. Ramsey replied that such procedures indeed do not cure a woman's infertility — that would seem to call for reconstructive surgery of some kind — but rather produce a child as a result of technology without affecting the woman's ability to conceive. "*In vitro* fertilization is not a medical procedure," he said. "It is manufacture by biological technology, not medicine."

Dr. Ramsey also warned that medical science may find itself called upon not only to produce children on demand, but also certain types of children, selected as to sex, color of hair, intelligence, or talent. At the same time, he praised the 1951 pronouncement against human artificial insemination made by Pope Pius XII, that ". . . to reduce the conjugal (marriage) act to a mere organic function for the transmission of the germ of life would be to convert the domestic hearth, sanctuary of the family, into nothing more than a biological laboratory." Dr. Ramsey concluded: "It is a final irony to realize invasions will now be done on man that we are slowly learning not to do on other natural objects. In actual practice, minerals and vegetables may be more respected than human parenthood, and mankind may be ushered happily into Brave New World. There is no abatement of acceptance of the view that human parenthood can be taken apart and reassembled in Oxford, England, New York and Washington, D. C. And of course it follows that thereafter human nature has to be wrought in commercial firms bearing the name 'Genetic Laboratories, Inc.' in all our metropolitan centers. Before it is realized that the objective has ceased to be the treatment of a medical condition, it will be too late, and Huxley will have been proved true."

Others question whether cloning of certain individuals would have any value at all. Suppose, for instance, at some future date when science was more advanced than today, that biologists had access to the body of Leonardo da Vinci. Suppose the Renaissance genius's cells were preserved well enough to permit one or two to be removed by cloners. Each cell would, of course, contain da Vinci's entire genetic blueprint, which these future scientists could translate and then duplicate with the right combination and order of DNA chemicals. Would another da Vinci, grown from one of his preserved bone cells, be of any worth to us? Would this cloned da Vinci paint another Mona Lisa or create monumental sculpture? Would the qualities that the clone could *not* inherit — acquired knowledge, for instance — make the entire effort pointless? No one knows the answers to these hypothetical questions. Some might point out that a biological copy is not enough, that it is the environment, the circumstances, that make an individual what he or she is, or that determine his or her usefulness. Leonardo in the year 3000 A.D. might be like a bewildered Stone Age man, born too late to have his talent appreciated. Or, turned the other way around, he would be born too early if he were cloned into some future Stone Age world, where brute strength and animal instincts were more important than his sort of genius.

Some of this is not as farfetched as it sounds. There have been recent suggestions that body cells from selected individuals be preserved today, as sperm is preserved, to be thawed when scientists have the capability to map their DNA and reconstruct it artificially, or to transplant and regrow a nucleus into a copy of the original. But, again, whether a future generation would gain anything from a replicated Richard Nixon or Martin Luther King, Jr., or a few extra copies of the Beatles or Buckminster Fuller, would depend on a host of factors — including our values, our needs, and how far we have evolved as a society.

Besides these intriguing speculations and the ethical questions raised by Dr. Ramsey and his colleagues, there are other unresolved issues related to unorthodox methods of cloning and fertilization. Some have argued, for instance, that using sperm from an anonymous donor constitutes adultery on the part of the wife, even though the husband may grant permission. There was a case in Nice, France, recently, in which a court granted a husband's rejection of the paternity of a child born to his wife after artificial insemination. The woman said that her husband had consented to the procedure, but he denied it. Under French law, the court could have granted his rejection of fatherhood even if it were proven that he had consented. There is also the question of such a child's legitimacy. In a number of states, these children are considered illegitimate, or else their rights of inheritance are hazy at best. There are many unanswered questions, such as whether a child's knowledge that he or she has been artificially inseminated will have any future adverse effect on that child's emotions — or on the father's, who may some years later brood over his infertility, along with the fact that it was another man's sperm that impregnated his wife.

Whose baby would it be if an egg from one woman were fertilized in the laboratory and then carried to term by a "mother for hire"? How would this surrogate mother feel about giving up the child? If the offspring were born malformed, could the doctor be held responsible? What legal recourse would the child have? Should the parents be allowed to reject it because it didn't turn out as expected?

Suppose parents in a neighborhood or town decided they wanted more female babies than males? Or vice versa. What effect would this imbalance have on the family unit? If sexual contact were removed totally from the reproductive process in a particular case, would the resulting child be treated differently from a naturally conceived one? Would our ideas about parenthood change?

Consider the case, in 1976, of a man who advertised in the newspaper for a substitute mother to bear his child through artificial insemination. The man's story — told to a reporter from the *San Francisco Chronicle* on the condition that the name of the father and the mother-for-hire not be revealed — was as follows: The man said he chose artificial insemination because it would be immoral for him to have a child by sexual relations with another woman. (His own wife, of course, was not able to bear children.) Nearly two hundred women answered the man's request, each one agreeing to the father's stipulation that he was never to meet the mother of his child. Finally a woman was selected. She was described only as an attractive, blond, unmarried woman who had never had a child. A sample of the man's sperm was taken, and injected into the woman's uterus. The result was a baby girl who developed some medical problems at first, but later went home and did well. The man's wife, who was a bit skeptical at first, took the baby in as her own, according to the father. The substitute mother had faced the same sort of dubious reaction when she first told her boss at work and her co-workers what she was planning to do. The boss's immediate reaction was: "That sort of thing isn't going on in my office." He reportedly changed his mind when the woman convinced him that she was doing something good. The father's total expenses for the procedure amounted to about ten thousand dollars — seven thousand to the mother, and the rest for legal and medical fees.

The story raises several important ethical and legal questions. One might wonder, for instance, about the propriety of advertising for a surrogate mother in this way, and whether hiring one's body out to bear a child and then, in effect, selling that child, is moral. Was the husband's action selfish, inconsiderate of his wife? Would it have been better if the couple had adopted? Is the child considered illegitimate because father and natural mother were not married?

As you reflect on what you have read so far, ask yourself another important question: Should biologists continue their research in cloning and *in vitro* fertilization? In answering it now, reserve the right to change your mind when you finish this book.

5

Viruses
and Cancer

Just about everybody has heard of viruses, those tinier-
than-bacteria nuisances that have been blamed for virtually every animal and human ailment, from the sniffles to
cancer. The blame has not been entirely misplaced. Hundreds of viruses and viruslike particles have turned up in
insects, plants, animals, and people, and a great many of
them known to be associated with disease. Some are
direct causes of illness. Smallpox, yellow fever, polio,
measles, and flu have long been known to be caused by
viruses. So too are cold sores, troublesome little blisters
that plague almost everyone; and shingles, a painful skin
rash and nerve infection. Multiple sclerosis, a chronic disease of the nervous system, and rheumatoid arthritis, a
crippling disease of the joints, may also be caused by viruses. There is conclusive evidence that viruses are a
factor in the production of serious birth defects, and
though there is no actual proof that they cause cancer in
people, there is no doubt whatsoever that they do cause

the disease in animals, plants, fish, and birds, and that
they are very likely involved in the malignancy in humans.

Viruses are of interest not only because of their rela-
tionship to disease, but because, as it turns out, they are
made up of the same stuff as genes — DNA. Viruses also
are becoming valuable laboratory tools in studies involving gene manipulation, a role that may more than make
up for all the trouble they have caused for so many years.
We'll look at that in a moment, but first some background
on these ubiquitous agents that are found in all of earth's
living things.

To begin with, viruses are extremely small. They are
visible only with an electron microscope. Germs, of course,
may be viewed under an ordinary light microscope.
Years ago, before anyone was actually able to spot a virus,
about all that scientists could do was to inject substances
believed to contain one into an animal and wait for an
effect. Or they implanted the substances in a fertile
chicken egg and watched the changes on the developing
embryo. Back in 1910, Dr. Francis Peyton Rous, a New
York pathologist, injected chickens with a filtered liquid
made from a sarcoma — one of the two main types of
cancer — found in another chicken. He repeated his experiment several times, and each time the results were the
same: the injected chickens developed the sarcoma, proof
that the extract, filtered free of cells, carried a virus that
was capable of transmitting malignancy. Dr. Rous's experiment — regarded as highly significant today — met
with a good deal of skepticism at the time, because the
popular assumption was that the cancer cell itself was the
only agent that could transmit cancer.

A virus's skin is a tough envelope of protein. Packed
inside in coils is a nucleic acid, either DNA or RNA. But
despite this store of life's substance, a virus is incapable of

living by itself; it hovers in a sort of gray world between life and nonlife . . . until it gets into a living cell. Once inside, this agent that was used to a quiet, wallflower existence is suddenly transformed into a sometimes vicious parasite. Injecting its DNA into the cell it has invaded, the virus takes over the cell's machinery, including its instructions for normal duplication. Tricked by the virus's frantic commands, and with its own genetic information altered or blotted out, the hapless cell is either forced to manufacture thousands of new viruses instead of normal protein before destroying itself, or it is so transformed that it produces endless copies of its new, flawed self. The final result of this savage production of bad copies could be a cancer. If, for example, a virus gets into a blood cell, it could cause leukemia, a cancer of the blood-forming tissues; in a breast cell, it could cause a breast tumor.

Some viruses work their will speedily; others take up residence in our bodies, lying quietly until something — drugs, environmental pollutants, or some biochemical change — touches them off, triggering disease-causing changes in the cell's genetic instructions. Cancer viruses, like some slow-acting infectious viruses, may exist for years, maybe generations, in an animal or human before they signal their presence by the development of a malignancy or an infection. The slow-virus theory is one of cancer biology's most fascinating suppositions. Imagine that somewhere in our bodies, in some cell nucleus, there exists a gene or genes programmed to produce a virus that can make cells cancerous. This insidious system, according to the theory, has been handed down to us over generations, and will continue to be passed along to future offspring. Normally the system — with its so-called virogenes — is kept shut off by regulator genes. But every so often some external agent sets them off, and cancer begins to grow. This is but one of several cancer theories, and it should be remembered that the role of viruses in the disease is very complex. Just how a virus turns a normal cell into a cancerous one is the big question still facing researchers. If they could find the mechanism, or isolate a single cancer gene, they could take a giant step toward cancer prevention.

Thus far, science has not come up with a wonder drug to cure or even treat a disease caused by a virus. About the only known defense is a preventive vaccine made from one of the offending viruses, which makes the body produce disease-fighting antibodies. Some encouraging results, however, have been obtained recently with a substance known as interferon, a protective protein that is produced naturally by the body in response to an attack by viruses. It is often not available quickly enough or in large amounts, and scientists have been trying to find ways to get the body to boost its production.

A viral infection may not necessarily mean disease. Some viruses, in fact, do no harm at all, and others might create symptoms so mild that they go unrecognized. In fact, for every treated case of paralytic polio there have been many hundreds of cases of the disease that went unnoticed.

An intriguing idea is that someday viruses may be harnessed to actually treat disease; this could be done by using them to carry healthy replacement genes to cells that lack them and thus cause genetic defects. As researchers become more adept, it is not inconceivable that gene repair, through what is known as gene transfer, or gene grafting, will be added to the handbook of therapeutic techniques. There have already been several relatively successful attempts at viral gene therapy. In one case in Germany, two young retarded sisters were found to be suffering from an inherent disorder, characterized by a much higher than normal amount of an amino acid in their systems. The imbalance was caused by the lack of an enzyme called arginase. This enzyme, scientists also knew, was related to one produced by a virus named *Shope papilloma*. After much consultation, doctors decided to administer a dose of the virus in an effort to get it to produce the missing enzyme, which would, in turn, right the chemical imbalance. The girls received a small dose of the purified virus, a fraction of the amount that would have been given mice; there was no apparent effect. About a year later, the girls were given a larger dose, and this time there was a 20 percent drop in their abnormally high level of the amino acid. The disease was too widespread, however, and the treatment did not take. The doctor who performed the gene therapy was roundly criticized for experimenting with a method that, in effect, meant deliberately infecting someone with a virus. His response was that practicing medicine means taking calculated risks, that there was nothing else to be done for the sisters, and that injecting the virus was similar to using a live virus vaccine.

Another exercise in what might be termed viral genetics was reported by a group of scientists at the National Institutes of Health in Bethesda, Maryland, in 1971. Their work involved a disease known as galactosemia. In this disorder, lack of an enzyme prevents the body from using the milk sugar, galactose, properly. If the condition is untreated — treatment usually involves a milk-free diet to cut off the supply of galactose — retardation, cataracts, malnutrition, and death can result. What the NIH scientists did was take a specially developed virus called a phage, which is able to enter bacterial cells. This virus also contained the ingredients necessary to code for galactose. When the scientists cultured this virus with human cells lacking the essential enzyme, some of the genetic message packed in the virus was transmitted to the cells. The enzyme was produced, and the deficiency corrected. While such gene insertion is not yet being used to treat galactosemia — diet is still the most practical method — there are important long-term implications of the work for genetic engineering.

Viruses have also been used to fight cancer by being made to stimulate a patient's weakened immune system, the system that defends us against disease. Back in 1950, for example, Dr. Alice E. Moore of New York's Sloan-Kettering Cancer Institute inoculated cancer patients with an agent called West Nile virus. She was able to shrink some of the tumors with the treatment. Unfortunately, a number of the patients came down with encephalitis, a virus-caused central nervous system disease. The patients recovered from encephalitis, but the research work with the virus was halted.

Another attempt at getting a virus to alter cells, so that the patient's own immune system attacks a tumor, was reported a few years ago by a group from St. Thomas Hospital in London. They injected terminally ill patients with a "friendly" virus named MP and watched their tumors and other types of cancer go into remission for as long as a year and a half. (Remission is a term that means the symptoms of a disease go away. Sometimes the remission is permanent, sometimes temporary; sometimes it is brought about by treatment, while other times it seems to occur for no apparent reason.)

If our immune system could be shored up or altered in some way, it might well be the key to warding off a wide range of diseases, even the aging process. Already, as we have seen, it can be prodded into destroying cancers. A virus is not always needed to do this, however. Dr. Edmund Klein of Roswell Park Memorial Institute in Buffalo and Dr. Issac Djerassi of Mercy Catholic Medical Center in Philadelphia have brought about dramatic improvement in a relatively small number of patients, with daily injections of massive amounts of germ-destroying white blood cells, called monocytes. Emphasizing that their findings are not yet a practical treatment for cancer, but merely a model to demonstrate a research principle, the two scientists told a recent American Cancer Society Science Writers' seminar of the development, by Dr. Djerassi, of a machine that over a four-hour period can extract billions of monocytes from healthy donors by trapping them on a nylon filter. Injected into fifteen patients with cancers that had spread from internal organs to the surface of the skin, the monocytes brought about either a decrease in size or complete disappearance of the surface cancers in all of the patients within hours or days. Continuing injections of the monocytes were required to prevent the tumors from recurring, the scientists reported. They added that the research was too preliminary to determine whether the white-cell therapy has any effect on internal tumors that cause skin lesions. It is also not yet known whether the injected monocytes kill the cancer cells directly, or whether they trigger the production of new monocytes at the site of the cancer.

In 1976 a group of scientists in New Orleans discovered that injection of a chemical substance called glucan — obtained from the walls of yeast cells — starts up powerful body defenses that block the start and spread of transplanted tumors in experimental animals. Where a transplanted tumor was already growing, glucan was able to block its growth, inhibit its spread to other tissues, or cause it to be totally rejected by the animals. Because of these experiments, the research team, headed by Dr. Nicholas DiLuzio, professor and chairman of the physiology department at Tulane University School of Medicine, proposed a new theory about the body's primary defense against cancer. It was their belief that amoebalike scavenger cells in the bloodstream called macrophages — not the white blood cells — were responsible for the destruction of tumor cells. The Tulane scientists' research, in fact, showed that glucan stimulated the multiplication and cell-devouring activity of these macrophages. They found that when they injected leukemia cells into mice and then inoculated them with glucan to stimulate macrophage production — or when they gave the animals glucan before they got the leukemia cells — development of the blood cancer in the host animal was blocked. Other kinds of cancer were also blocked effectively by glucan injection. In rats, growth of one form of tumor was reduced by 76 percent and growth of another by 69 percent in twenty-one days. Again, inhibition of tumor growth was associated with glucan-induced multiplication of bacteria-destroying macrophages. In all the experiments, normal body cells were "ignored" by the macrophages.

It is the feeling of some scientists that as the immune system declines with age, its white cells mutate and these genetic misfits attack perfectly normal cells because they don't recognize them as friendly. Or it might be that the body's defenders turn against its own mutant cells, viewing them as "not self" because of their genetically altered makeup. The result of all this internal warfare, it is theorized, is the deterioration and destruction of the body, the process we know as aging. Dr. Takashi Makinodan, of the Gerontology Research Center in Baltimore, removed white cells from young rats and injected them into older rats, boosting their resistance to disease and enabling them to withstand ordinarily fatal doses of disease-carrying bacteria. In other experiments, he found that by injecting spleen cells from younger mice, the life-span of a mouse can be lengthened by nearly a third. (The spleen, a lymph organ located in the upper portion of the abdomen, disposes of spent red blood cells and manufactures monocytes.) The results of this combined research suggest that old cells require more frequent stimulation if they are to continue to produce antibodies at the same rate as young cells. The implications are that with proper stimulation an older animal, a category that includes humans, can be made as resistant to certain types of diseases as a younger one normally is.

While it has not yet been tried in humans, the work of Dr. Makinodan and others suggests that one day disease-fighting cells might be removed from a person when young and healthy, frozen at below-zero temperatures, and then reinjected in later life.

All of the experiments that have been described thus far sound a lot easier than they actually are. For example, one cannot simply inject a missing enzyme to correct a genetic defect. Getting the enzyme to the proper site in the body is a formidable task in itself. But even more difficult is stopping the body's immune defenses from rejecting and destroying the foreign enzyme that has been introduced. In kidney transplants, potent drugs called immunosuppressives are administered to the graft recipient. These drugs weaken the defenses so that the system will not fight the grafted kidney. Unfortunately, with the immune system down, every harmful kind of bacteria and virus, along with the transplant, is left unhindered.

With regard to enzyme injection, some scientists have been experimenting with ways to "trick" cells into accepting an enzyme. What they do, basically, is package the enzyme in minuscule fatty spheres called liposomes, which, in turn, are coated with a substance that fools the immune system into letting the enzyme package get through. In this chemical disguise, the enzyme slips by to take its place in a deficient cell where, hopefully, it can right a genetic wrong.

Another experimental method of delivering a missing ingredient to cells uses sperm. As we said earlier, sperm fertilize egg cells. However, in 1974 scientists at Memorial Sloan-Kettering succeeded in uniting mouse sperm, not with eggs, but with body cells from a hamster. Electron micrographs depicted a rather startling scene: the DNA-laden heads of the sperm were buried in the hamster cells, but their tails protruded outside. Analysis of the penetrated cells turned up evidence of proteins normally present in mouse fetuses, an indication that the mouse sperm had manufactured a gene product in the hamster cell. Commented Dr. Aaron Bendich: "There must be more than six hundred well-established genetic diseases, many of them characterized by the absence of normal genes. I think it should be possible to correct some of these deficiencies, at some future time, by administering sperm to cells taken from diseased individuals, getting the sperm to deliver some of the missing DNA, allowing the cell to build up into a healthy population and reimplanting them in the patient."

Bacteria too are being harnessed in the laboratory for useful purposes. A genetically engineered strain of germs called *Pseudomonas,* for instance, is being "trained" to devour environmental pollutants, such as oil spills in the ocean, much as ordinary bacteria get rid of dead animals and plants through decomposition and change them into soil-enriching substances. The work cut out for *Pseudomonas* is a lot like that of the scavenger macrophages, which, as we saw earlier, battle cancer cells. There is another side of the coin to consider, however. What if an oil-eating *Pseudomonas* somehow got loose in an oil storage depot, an airplane, an auto lubrication system, or the tanks that feed our home furnaces?

Bacteria also help in digestion, and they break down the waste matter in our sewers. The bacteria in the sewer sludge, in fact, may one day do what an artificial kidney does for victims of kidney disease — sop up the poisonous wastes in human systems. Scientists from the Cleveland Clinic Foundation reported in 1976 that they have already used sewer bacteria to remove such waste products as urea and creatinine from laboratory samples of urine. "These recent studies indicate the ability of mixed species of bacteria to utilize known urinary constituents in quantities approaching those required in the treatment of kidney failure," Dr. Paul S. Malchesky told the Twenty-ninth Annual Conference on Engineering and Medicine and Biology, in Boston. "The question of whether or not mixed strains of microorganisms can be developed to substitute for renal [kidney] function cannot be answered at this time, but it is believed that this concept offers a fresh approach to the problems encountered with present therapies."

Nearly twenty-five thousand people in the United States rely on the artificial-kidney machine for chronic renal support. Such machines carry blood outside the body and wash away the wastes before returning it to the patient's circulation. To support a large-scale program of kidney dialysis, the American working public pays over a million dollars a day.

"The impetus," said Malchesky, "is therefore to reduce the high cost of this growing program. Even more important, however, is the need to make the renal substitute more physiologic. In order to approach the goal of a more physiologic process, the idea of utilizing microorganisms was conceived."

If this idea ever becomes workable in patients, the speculation is that the bacteria might be mixed with the blood outside the body, taken orally in pill form, or injected into the system where they would, in effect, "eat up" the waste products.

6

Regeneration

As was mentioned earlier, a little-understood "on-off" mechanism in a gene decides which cells become what, and produces birth defects or cancer by turning on the right (or wrong) genes. If some way could be found to govern that switch — that is, to control the process of cell differentiation — we might be able to prevent a broad range of human ailments, maybe even grow new organs or limbs in people to replace lost or diseased ones.

Recently the University of Chicago's Dr. Charles Huggins and a colleague, Haridara Reddi, reported that they had discovered an electrochemical method of working the "on-off" switch. Using bone matrix — a protein that is able to change soft fibrous cells called fibroblasts to cartilage, bone, and bone marrow, in a sort of biological chain reaction — the researchers stopped or started cell differentiation in adult rats. They did this by changing the electrical charge on the material. In their experiments, bone matrix (which remains behind after the powdered bone that contains it is "demineralized" by being treated with an acid) was placed beneath the skin of rats. Within twenty-four hours, Dr. Huggins reported, the genetic program of the rat's fibroblast tissue was changed. Not only were there new enzymes, but everything began occurring according to a timetable. "On day seven," said Dr. Huggins, "you find cartilage, on day eleven you find bone, and on day eighteen you find bone marrow. This procedure is reminiscent of embryonic differentiation in humans and other mammals, whereby from the fertilized ovum appear over a hundred cells, each with a different program." By treating the bone matrix with an electrochemical that put a positive charge on it, the researchers were able to give it tissue-transforming power; by treating the matrix with a substance carrying a negative charge, they halted the process. The Reddi-Huggins research refers back to a classic 1930 demonstration by Dr. Huggins, in which he transformed connective tissue in dogs directly into bone by imitating the process through which bones are formed in infant skulls. In 1965 another University of Chicago research group demonstrated that demineralized powdered bone and teeth will make connective tissue in experimental animals differentiate into cartilage, bone, and marrow in the same way that most skeletal bones are formed naturally.

More startling, however, is what scientists from Philadelphia's Institute of Cancer Research and from Oxford University have accomplished — actually growing mice from deadly cancer cells called teratomas. A report on how they redirected the cells was presented at a 1976 seminar at the Jackson Laboratory in Bar Harbor, Maine. A teratoma — which literally means "wonder tumor" — is a freakish growth of egg or sperm cells. Unlike other tumors, teratomas contain pieces of bone, muscle, skin, nerve, brain, heart, and other organs, even bits of teeth. But while these bits are clearly recognizable, they are mixed together in a misshapen mass that in no way resembles a normal embryo. The differentiation process is at work in the teratoma, producing all kinds of cells, but something has gone wrong with the chemical signal system that directs it, and wild growth results.

Amazingly, however, when scientists took these deadly tumors from mice and implanted a single cell from one of them into a normal embryo a few days after conception, the malignant cell quit its erratic behavior. What is more, the perfect baby mouse that was finally born out of this union of normal and malignant cells contained organs and tissues partly derived from the tumor and partly from the normal cells of two other parents. The resulting animal is called a chimera, after the mythical fire-breathing beast with a lion's head, goat's body, and serpent's tail. Scientists have nicknamed their chimera, this mouse whose parents include a killer cancer cell, Terry Tom. They don't know exactly what it was that switched off the cancer and ordered it to change to normal mouse tissue. Speculation centers, for the moment, on some chemical in the normal mouse embryo. Commented one researcher who attended the seminar: "What Terry Tom has taught us is that if you put cancer cells into the right environment, they stop being cancer cells." Terry Tom has since sired many other apparently normal mice who, in turn, are producing more mice. Each, of course, has organs that are descended in part from the teratoma. Scientists are interested in Terry Tom, his children and grandchildren because they are ideal models for studying the mystery of cell differentiation. If science can decipher the signals that can turn teratomas into healthy mouse tissue, it will have a solid clue to what makes cancer cells run out of control. Then they might be able to use that knowledge to benefit human beings. As Dr. Leroy C. Stevens, a scientist at the Jackson Laboratory, put it. "Perhaps instead of trying to kill cancer cells, we can find a way of turning them on to doing normal, useful things, just the way teratomas are somehow turned on to becoming normal mouse tissues."

This leads us to regeneration, an organism's ability to repair itself by growing new parts. The notion that science might stimulate regeneration in mammals is not new. One man who thought long and hard on the prospect was Lazzaro Spallanzani (1729–1799), an Italian experimental biologist, who demonstrated, among other things, that microbes in food could be killed by boiling. Spallanzani was also the first person to observe isolated bacterial cells divide. With regard to regeneration, he wrote in 1768: "If frogs are able to renew their legs when young, why should they not do the same when farther advanced? Are the wonderful reproductions mentioned in the newts only to be ascribed to the effect of water, in which these animals were kept? This is contradicted in the instance of the salamander, whose parts were reproduced even on dry ground. But if the above-mentioned animals, either aquatic or amphibian, recover their legs when kept on dry ground, how comes it to pass that other land animals, such as are accounted perfect, and are better known to us, are not endowed with the same power? Is it to be hoped that they may acquire them by some useful dispositions?"

The questions are intriguing ones that are still asked by biologists interested in the formation, structure, and breakdown of tissues. Consider, for example, the remarkable hydra, a simple, multicellular, freshwater animal, which, despite its seemingly uncomplicated structure, has incredible powers of regeneration. Chopped into fairly large pieces, each piece develops into a complete new organism; small bits of hydra, when placed close together, re-form into another hydra. Why does this happen? Why also do salamanders and crabs grow new limbs when the old ones are amputated? A salamander has in its limbs the same structures that we do — five fingers, muscles, bones, joints, nerves, cartilage, and skin. When one of its limbs is severed, the cells in the stump do not appear to die as they do in a human limb. Instead of scar tissue being formed, a sac grows over the stump, preventing the exposed cells from escaping. But in humans, a severed limb is prevented from regenerating by the scar that forms, and about all that we seem to be able to do is renew hair, nails, skin, and portions of the liver, and repair bone fractures and wounds.

Regeneration is, of course, a cellular process that is regulated by a highly sophisticated control system. Electrical activity probably plays an important part in it. Present in both plant and animal cells, electricity controls the beating of the heart, the contraction of muscles, and the activity of the brain. It is also associated with growth and the repair of injuries. Experiments along the lines of those performed by Dr. Huggins, Dr. Robert O. Becker, and Dr. Joseph A. Spadaro of the State University of New York's Upstate Medical Center, have led to the theory that if cells and tissues had electrochemical properties, then tiny electrical currents might act as control signals. They implanted a small electric device in the upper portion of a rat's leg — the lower part had been severed — and switched on an electric current. The result of the simple experiment far exceeded the scientists' expectations. They managed to bring about partial regeneration of the severed rat limb. The experiment achieved a replacement of skeletal muscle along with the bone growth.

Also, a mass of cells known as a blastema was formed. Such a mass consists of young, undifferentiated cells at the outset; later the blastema differentiates into a wide range of cell types necessary to replace a missing part. True regenerative growth starts with the formation of such a blastema — and since the scientists were able to form one, they knew that their experiment was successful.

Similarly, a scientist at Columbia University Hospital recently developed a technique to successfully promote bone regeneration in children with congenital pseudarthrosis, an affliction also known as "false joint." This results from the failure of fractured bone ends to unite. As we saw in the experiment involving the severed rat leg, scientists have had some luck either in healing a bone fracture or in achieving partial regeneration by implanting electrodes in the bone and stimulating the area with an electrical current. Dr. Andrew Bassett of Columbia, however, has been able to regenerate bone in five children without electrode implantation. Each child had previously undergone several operations in attempts to rejoin the bone ends, but to no avail. Dr. Bassett had casts placed on the children's affected legs, and then inserted a pair of coils into each cast, one on either side of the break. He then "pulsed" the coils with twenty-four to thirty volts, creating a magnetic field near the site of the fracture. In all five children, satisfactory union of the breaks was achieved. Even though the healing mechanism of electromagnetic action is unclear, researchers believe that the method may ultimately be applied to routine fractures and may reduce healing time by as much as 50 percent.

Armed with the answer to the regeneration question, researchers might well be on the way to understanding more about a number of diseases, and to fulfilling a prediction made a few years ago by Dr. James Bonner of the

California Institute of Technology. He declared that if a cell's genetic program could be reset, scientists might be able to prolong life by encouraging a cell or group of cells to turn into a new organ. A cell with its DNA programmed for, say, a heart or a kidney might be cultured in a laboratory hothouse, then reimplanted in two or three years when the new organ was fully grown and the old one was showing signs of failing. Rejection, the problem that bothers organ transplants, would not occur, since the cells from which the new tissue was grown would not be foreign to the recipient. Theoretically, at least, one could replace any defective organ simply by growing a new one when the time came. "It is probably safe to assume that every organ has the power to regrow lying latent within it," former Harvard anatomist Marcus Singer said a few years ago, "needing only the appropriate 'useful dispositions' to bring it out."

The liver is one of the best examples of this potential for organ regeneration. For years, it has been known that, when as much as 80 or even 90 percent of the liver is surgically removed from an experimental animal, virtually the entire organ will regrow. This remarkable process also occurs in humans, often with amazing speed, as long as the small amount of liver left after resection has an adequate blood supply. A few years ago, Dr. Jan K. Siemsen, a radiologist at the University of Southern California, scanned a number of patients at Los Angeles County–USC Medical Center who had had large portions of their livers cut out. All of the patients regrew a normal-sized, functioning liver; in one case, the organ regenerated in a week, while the others took only up to two weeks. Dr. Siemsen also found that the larger the portion of liver removed, the quicker the organ regrew; in some cases where a small portion was removed, there was no regrowth. Furthermore, the organ regenerated no matter which area of it was removed, and it did so without any outside means of stimulation. The process simply occurred as a natural bodily function.

The reason resected livers regenerate has been under investigation for some time, and, while the issue is not yet settled, all the available evidence seems to point toward a hormone present in the circulatory system that supplies the pancreas or duodenum. (The pancreas, located in back of the stomach, makes fat-digesting enzymes and the hormone insulin. The duodenum is the upper part of the small intestine.) Confirmation that a governing factor exists in the blood has come from investigators at the University of California in San Diego. In a series of experiments, they removed rats' livers and then returned them to their owners, but to other sites, arranging the vein system in several different ways. The result was that only the livers tied to a portal blood supply (veins leading from the intestines into the liver) regrew. Later the San Diego team virtually isolated the source of the blood factor presumed responsible for the regrowth. At the 1974 meeting of the American College of Surgeons, they reported on experiments in which they grafted livers along with specific organs from the gastrointestinal tract. They found that only the liver grafts that got their blood supply from the pancreas — or the pancreas in conjunction with the duodenum — regrew; livers transplanted with only the duodenum or small intestine did not. The pancreas thus appears to be the origin of the regenerating factor.

Working in another vital area, scientists at the University of Chicago recently developed a way to isolate, grow, and replicate adult human heart cells. Earlier they had grown heart cells taken from adult rats. If the mechanism that regulates such regrowth could be manipulated by physicians, they might be able to restore damaged heart muscle after a heart attack. All the existing evidence up until the Chicago work had suggested that human, rat, or chicken muscle cells ceased to divide soon after birth and could not regenerate new muscle in the adult after injury. While the Chicago findings are still preliminary, they could conceivably lead not only to improved methods for regrowing heart muscle after heart attack or cardiac surgery, but also to the formation of heart cell banks from which surgeons could draw healthy muscle to replace dead or scarred tissue.

Scientists have also found out how to generate human blood cells outside the body — using a living mouse as the "factory." Human blood cells originate within the bone marrow in a highly complicated process at the rate of hundreds of billions a day. Half of our ten or so pints of blood consists of an amber fluid called plasma. The blood cells, red and white — along with colorless, disk-shaped particles called platelets — are suspended in the plasma. There are some thirty trillion red cells in a human being, each one carrying hemoglobin, the pigment that transports oxygen. There are fewer white cells, somewhere on the order of one for every eight hundred red cells. These compose the body's defense system. Platelets, important in the formation of clots that close up bleeding vessels after an injury, number about one and a half trillion.

The "mouse-factory" system of continually growing human blood cells was devised a few years ago at the Brookhaven National Laboratory, by a team headed by Dr. Eugene P. Cronkite, chairman of the laboratory's medical department. What the scientists did was construct a device called a diffusion chamber. The sides of the chamber were made of fine filter paper, with openings too small for cells to escape from, but large enough to let fluid in. Human bone marrow cells, which form blood, were placed in the chamber, which was then implanted inside the mouse's abdominal cavity. There it floated, surrounded by all the vital fluids and nutrients necessary for cell growth. In a few weeks, millions of cells were grown in this living laboratory, each one eventually differentiating into the various types found in normal marrow.

Not only does this chamber system enable scientists to study more closely the complex blood-forming activities that go on deep inside the marrow, but it might ultimately lead to improved treatment of blood diseases by providing more information about their origin. The chamber method may also be used someday to provide marrow for transplant in such diseases as leukemia, a cancer of the blood-forming tissue, and anemia, a disease marked by a deficiency of red blood cells.

The search for ways to study the defects in the body's regulatory system that touch off blood diseases such as leukemia is not new. In the 1800s, the famous Russian scientist Elie Metchnikoff suggested using a porous bag in which to grow blood cells as a means of studying how they work. His technique was not successful. Until the Brookhaven experiment, all of the attempts had failed because they did not match the body's own process closely enough to allow growth of all cell types.

Another idea that has intrigued scientists is the development of artificial blood — some substance that would replace the blood cells and the protein in plasma. Several laboratories have been working on such a substitute. At the Harvard School of Public Health, a few years ago, Dr. Robert P. Geyer was able to keep rats alive for a time with nothing in their veins but a solution of semiorganic compounds called fluorocarbons, and synthetic chemicals known as emulsifiers. Scientists still have a long way to go, however, before the blood substitute can be tested in human patients.

As you think about what has been said in this chapter about cell regeneration, you might get the impression that cells that are able to reproduce do so indefinitely, that they are, in effect, immortal. This does not appear to be true. Cells, as explained earlier, reproduce by dividing in two, and then again and again. Some divide more quickly than others. Thousands of new skin cells, for example, may be formed every day to replace those damaged or destroyed by injuries or disease; red blood cells and epithelial cells (those that line the intestines) are renewed in a few days or months. Heart and limb muscle cells renew at a slower pace, while liver cells hardly ever divide unless a portion of the organ is removed. Other cells, like those in the brain and the rest of the nervous system, do not appear to be able to reproduce themselves. (These brain and nervous-system cells begin to die at the startling rate of some one hundred thousand a day when we are in our late twenties, but there are billions in every one of us from birth, and we seem to withstand the loss well.)

The process of cell growth and cell death, then, is carefully regulated so that cell count is kept within clear-cut limits. It is a good thing this is so. If, for instance, the fetus's phenomenal growth during the second three months of pregnancy were allowed to continue without nature's check on it, at maturity it would cover the earth. For years biologists believed that human cells could be put in a culture dish in a laboratory, nourished, and be made to replicate endlessly. The noted French surgeon, experimental biologist, and 1912 Nobel Prize winner Alexis Carrel — who played a leading role in the development of a new technique for suturing blood vessels, and who was a pioneer in organ transplantation and safe blood transfusion — was among those convinced by the early experiments that cultured cells could indeed multiply forever. Carrel apparently managed to keep chicken heart cells in culture continually growing and multiplying for nearly thirty-five years; he did this by feeding them a chicken embryo extract. He intentionally ended his experiment in 1939, calculating that if he hadn't destroyed some of his growing culture each day, it would have engulfed the earth's surface in twenty years.

In 1907 a German researcher named Paul Ehrlich started a culture of mouse tumor cells that thrives today in laboratories throughout the world, seemingly immortal. But the classic example of a long-thriving human cell line had its beginning in 1951, with cells obtained from the cervix (the neck of the uterus) of a young woman with cancer. The woman, who ultimately died of the disease, was given the pseudonym Helen Lane; the cells, which continue to grow and divide in many laboratories and are used in numerous research projects, are known as the HeLa strain. The first human cancer sample to multiply in culture, HeLa cells have proved to be one of the hardiest and most studied human strains.

But the notion that cells are immortal has been challenged by scientists, notably Dr. Leonard Hayflick of Stanford University School of Medicine. He has come up with the best evidence that a "genetic clock" in our cells' DNA regulates the rate at which our cells grow — and the pace at which we age. Hayflick has suggested that the chicken embryo extract that Carrel fed regularly to his "immortal" culture contained some fresh living cells, and that this was the reason the cultures grew as they did for so many years. It has been suggested further that the reason the other long-lived cell lines, like those from Ehrlich's mouse and Helen Lane, have continued to replicate indefinitely is because they were abnormal to begin with, that is, cancerous. Normally, as we have noted, cells have forty-six chromosomes; but the HeLa cells were found to contain from fifty to three hundred and fifty chromosomes. The malignancy, according to this line of reasoning, stops the biological clock of aging at the same time it drastically alters the mechanism that directs normal cell growth; the cells, ironically, attain immortality, but the price is a fatal disease, cancer, for their owner. Says Hayflick: "There may be a specific gene carrying a specific program of aging, or a sequence of genes at the end of the DNA strand, which says, in effect, 'That's enough. Let's start closing things down now.'"

In an important experiment in 1961, Hayflick, then at the Wistar Institute in Philadelphia, laid to rest the general belief that cells in tissue culture are ageless. Removing cells from the lung tissue of a four-month-old human embryo, he cultured them and discovered that they doubled about fifty times, then stopped. Cells taken from the lung tissue of a twenty-year-old man, on the other hand, multiplied about twenty times before slowing down and dying. Next Hayflick decided to find out whether cells had a "memory" — that is, whether they could "recall" the number of times they had doubled. He froze some of his cell colonies in liquid nitrogen at different stages — after, say, ten or twenty doublings — thus stopping their biological clocks and the divisions. Amazingly, when the cells thawed, they resumed dividing — with each colony taking up exactly where it had left off, multiplying only as many times as remained from its original program. For example, cells that had been frozen and stored at the twentieth doubling went on to divide about thirty more times before they quit. Furthermore, the cells "remembered" the doubling level they had reached before storage, even after a deep freeze that had lasted for as long as ten years.

Hayflick also found that the number of cell doublings is related to the life-span of the species. Mouse cells, for instance, divide about twelve times, while those from a chicken, which lives many years longer than a mouse, divide around twenty-five times. The number of doublings also seems to be related to the age of the cell donor, with fewer divisions the older the donor.

It is widely believed that "Hayflick's limit," as it is called, can be applied to many different body cells, and that the events that have happened in laboratory culture dishes also occur in people and other animals. Many feel, then, that the limit holds *in vivo* and *in vitro*, and that human beings are programmed to live no longer than the uppermost limit of their species. The 115 or so years that humans can live roughly represents the time required for our cells to undergo the maximum fifty divisions.

Transplant experiments have also lent support to the limiting characteristics of cells. A team from the University of California in Santa Cruz transplanted mouse cells into mice of a similar genetic background, and found that the cells gradually lost their ability to multiply with repeated grafting. Animal tumors, on the other hand, can be transplanted indefinitely, and there are some that have survived since the early 1900s, evidence that in cases of malignancy, such as in HeLa cells, cells may be "immortal."

The limit on normal human cell growth does not necessarily mean that science will never be able to do anything about it. The aging process can even now be slowed a bit — at least in a test tube — by altering the cell's environment with drugs and chemicals. Other laboratory approaches are aimed at manufacturing genes that will both slow the aging process and obliterate genetically transmitted disease. A logical step would be to synthesize — or possibly transplant from a younger person to an older one — hardier genetic material. The "wrong" DNA, therefore, could be "edited out" and replaced by a better program for a longer, healthier life. How scientists have successfully synthesized genes — and even gotten them to function as natural genes do — is the subject of the next chapter.

7

Artificial Genes

In 1969 a group of young scientists at Harvard Medical School did something that made headlines for molecular genetics. They separated pure, clearly defined genes from a living organism, an achievement that would make it easier for other scientists to study how these minuscule units of inheritance go about their business. Up till this time, scientists had been hampered in their examination of the intricate cellular mechanisms because the genes they wished to work with were invariably mixed together with other genes.

The work of the Harvard researchers was quite complicated. In fact, one of them told a reporter rather facetiously, "Sometimes I don't even understand it myself." It might be likened to removing only tiny bits of, say, parsley from a vegetable soup.

The research revolved around a species of bacteria called *Escherichia coli*, or *E. Coli*, for short. *E. coli* is a common germ found in the intestines of humans and animals, and it is as popular a laboratory-test subject as Drosophila, the fruit fly. The genes the scientists isolated were of the type called *lac operon*, which determines how the bacteria use a sugar, lactose.

To isolate the pure genes, the scientists used bacterial viruses called bacteriophages, agents that are capable of extracting various genes from the bacteria. Once the genes were sucked into the bacterial virus, the researchers went about the difficult task of separating the ones they wanted from the rest of the genes in the "soup mix." They did this with an enzyme that digested only the unwanted portion of the DNA, leaving the strand of genetic material they were after. A few years before, Dr. Max Birnstiel and his co-workers at the Institute of Animal Genetics in Edinburgh, Scotland, had also succeeded in isolating a unit of heredity, this one from an African clawed toad, the genetic system of which more closely resembles a human's than does *E. coli*'s. This was the first reported separation of a gene. The Harvard team's achievement, according to the American scientists, was the first time pure genes — that is, genes free from other genetic material — had been isolated. Both accomplishments have, of course, paved the way toward a better understanding of genes' behavior and the role they play in defects and disease. There are practical possibilities of another kind. What if scientists could separate the gene that directs the manufacture of silk in a silkworm? Or, if they could isolate the gene responsible for making the essential hormone insulin? Inserted into a bacterium, or into a host of bacteria, such a gene might be stimulated into producing large quantities of the substance for which it is coded. The bacteria would be transformed into busy minifactories, producing insulin to treat diabetes.

This sort of work, as we have cautioned throughout the

book, could also be misused. In fact, the Harvard team that isolated the *E. coli* gene expressed a good deal of concern over what they had done. One of the scientists, Dr. Jonathan R. Beckwith, said at the time: "The more we thought about it, the more we thought about the possibility that this particular set of steps might be used the wrong way. I think it is rather obvious that the work could lead to genetic engineering. The steps are not existent now, but when one stops to think about it, with work in higher organisms, it is not inconceivable that in not too long a time this sort of technique could be used. The more you think about it, the more it becomes frightening. In fact, it's more frightening than hopeful. Of course, there are beneficial aspects here. The way things have been going up to now, however, I'm afraid that the bad is going to far outweigh the good."

Why, then, do it?

One of the other team members, Dr. James Shapiro, explained it this way: "We did this work for scientific reasons. Also, because it was interesting to do. But scientists generally have the tendency to not think too much about the consequences of their work while doing it. But now that we have, we are not entirely happy about it. This is a problem in all scientific research, the bad consequences we cannot control. Many of us are upset that science and technology have been used, as in Vietnam, on innocent people. I don't think we necessarily have the right to pat ourselves on the back."

Not every scientist, we might add, holds that opinion. Some see only the potential benefits of DNA research, defending it on the basis of the lives that might be saved or improved through its pursuit. Some argue that it is part of human nature to be curious, to probe the unknown for scientific knowledge.

Much of the controversy that swirls about genetic engineering focuses on a form of research called recombinant DNA studies. In this work, one kind of genetic material is combined with another kind of DNA from a different organism, and the result is something that may not have existed in nature before. This type of research will be discussed in the next chapter. But for the moment let's turn to the step that follows separation of a gene. This is synthesis, the manufacture of artificial DNA by scientists working with the very chemicals contained in the original, natural gene.

In 1970 an artificial gene was made for the very first time by Nobel laureate Har Gobind Khorana, who was then at the University of Wisconsin and now works at the Massachusetts Institute of Technology. Khorana's was a yeast gene, but not enough was known then about its biochemical controls, the "start-stop" signals that enable a cell's machinery to utilize the coded information in various processes. Later the MIT group synthesized a bacterial gene with the potential to function in a living cell. Finally, in 1976 came the exciting news from Dr. Khorana's team — they had made the first synthetic gene that was fully functional in a living organism. This meant that the scientists were able to construct from ordinary laboratory chemicals not only the gene but its "start-stop" mechanism as well.

The gene that they laboriously synthesized by "stitching" together the chemical units that compose DNA and gluing them to an enzyme is called tyrosine transfer RNA. It is found naturally in *E. coli* bacteria, and one of its functions is to correct a harmful mutation that can occur in natural genes. Genes plagued with such a mutation create nonfunctional, incomplete proteins. The scientists took their man-made gene, complete with its control signals, and introduced it into a bacterium aboard a virus. Inside the bacterium that contained a mutant gene, which was stopping the production of protein, the artificial gene did exactly what was expected of it — it canceled out the "stop" signal so that normal proteins could be produced. This synthetic gene has been built to do good, and it may someday enable scientists to manipulate the biology of a living system to erase genetic defects or other abnormal characteristics. Since many human genetic abnormalities involve a deficiency in protein, an artificial gene that makes healthy protein would obviously be a valuable tool. "What we can do now is repair genetic defects in a tiny organism," Dr. Hans-Joachim Fritz, one of Dr. Khorana's team, said recently. "The obvious conclusion is that we might be able to do that someday in a larger one. But we do have a long way to go to reach that point."

It is true that the benefits to be derived from the MIT work are not going to be felt right away. The synthesis is just the beginning step in the investigation of that particular gene. Scientists interested in synthesizing a human gene have some formidable obstacles to overcome. One of the most difficult is a matter of scale: the typical human gene measures millions of units, while *E. coli's* is only about two hundred units long. Furthermore, it has been estimated that the chances of getting a virus to transport the right piece of DNA into a cell, using the easiest method known, are about one in one hundred thousand. And even if the DNA does get in, no one really knows how many of an ailing individual's cells have to be so treated to cure a disease or defect. These problems will undoubtedly be resolved. Just when, however, is anyone's guess.

8

The Problem of Recombinant DNA

After Dr. Khorana succeeded in synthesizing the *E. coli* gene, he was quick to point out that what he and his team had done was very different from the controversial work involving recombinant DNA — the joining together of DNA from different organisms. "In our work, there is no risk whatsoever," he said. "We are dealing with a completely defined system, containing a single gene which is already present in, and absolutely necessary to, all living cells."

To that, Dr. Fritz added: "The technique we used was similar to that used in recombinant DNA studies. But it is different in that we never ever introduced any foreign genetic information into an organism. We built a gene from the chemical ingredients that make up that gene in nature and put it into the organism in which it is found."

Work on recombinant DNA and the experiments that are associated with it have touched off much heated debate both within and outside the scientific community. Recall that the principal ingredient of the heredity-bearing genes is the spiral-staircase molecule, DNA. The arrangement of its chemical rungs and sides, as we have seen, is what determines its own special genetic code and, therefore, what each cell will be and do. Moreover, as noted, ordinary DNA is packed in the nucleus of every living cell. Using that background, the controversy can be more clearly understood.

In the 1950s, biologists discovered something that would pave the way for DNA-recombining experiments. They found that the genetic material was present not only in the chromosomes in the nuclei of cells, but in other parts of the cells as well. For example, DNA was detected in chloroplasts in green plants. Chloroplasts are "power plants" located outside the cell's nucleus; they do the job of photosynthesis, the process by which plants convert light from the sun directly into chemical energy. DNA also exists in a cell's mitochondria — "powerhouses" that provide the cell's energy by converting sugar and fats into fuel. Finally, DNA is present in tiny, circular particles called plasmids that float free in the cells of bacteria.

Since these DNA types are not confined within the walls of the nucleus, nor caught up in the hum of its complex machinery, scientists can get at them fairly easily. This is particularly true of plasmids. They are not only accessible but they also handle well in the laboratory and — this last point is most important — can slip easily into other bacteria. There they reside comfortably, dividing and redividing as their bacterium host divides and redivides.

Another important discovery in the DNA experiments was the purification of a special enzyme that has been likened to a chemical scalpel, because it can cut the delicate DNA into neat pieces. Without this chemical knife — called a restriction enzyme — attempts to break up DNA would undoubtedly result in ruining it beyond repair.

There is something else about this restriction enzyme. When it is used to slice up DNA, the pieces it produces have sticky ends. This means that when a specific bit of DNA is cut out of a plasmid from a bacterium and then mixed with DNA cut, let us say, from a virus, the sticky ends of each DNA piece glue together. It makes little difference that the DNA sources are different, bacterium or virus. The point is that something new has been constructed. After the two bits of DNA are fused into one, this tiny new genetic package, now known as recombinant DNA, may be easily introduced into bacteria. As the bacteria multiply by division, each new cell that is produced contains recombinant DNA that is exactly the same as that made when the original was glued together. So simple is the technique that any one of you could do it, as long as you or your school chemistry laboratory had some of the enzyme.

Therefore, genes from just about any living organism can be transferred to cells of completely unrelated organisms. In addition to transferring genes from one species of bacterium to another, scientists have also introduced genes from rabbits, toads, fruit flies, and other living things into *E. coli*. This means that probably any kind of gene from any kind of organism could find a home in *E. coli*. For the first time, science can take genetic material from two different sources, join it, and then grow as much of it as desired. This will enable cell biologists to scrutinize genes as never before, increasing their understanding of basic biological processes. As a U.S. government report on recombinant DNA has put it: "Now, for the first time, there is a way to cross very large evolutionary boundaries, and for moving genes between organisms that are believed to have previously had little genetic contact."

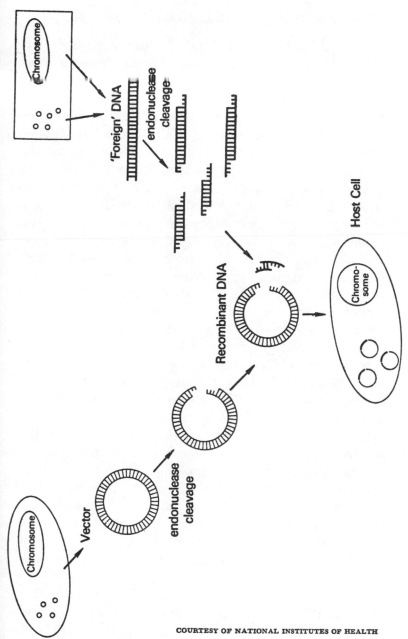

Recombinant DNA. DNA from one source is combined with DNA from another source, and then inserted into a host cell

All of this has quite naturally caused a good deal of excitement among biologists. Besides the chance to learn more about the structure of genes and how they work, the scientists foresee some very practical applications for medicine — particularly as it pertains to inherited disease — industry, and agriculture. Take the last, agriculture. Although plants are not animals — they cannot, for example, move from place to place, nor do they possess an immune system of white cells to ward off infectious disease — they are nevertheless alive. Plants are made up of cells and chromosomes, they require food, they grow organs and tissues, they develop diseases. The similarities are there, and animal-cell biologists look often to plants for clues about how or whether to tamper with a cell. Plant-cell biologists, on the other hand, look to animal biology for ways to improve laboratory techniques. Their work is more directly concerned with the quality and quantity of food supplies, and less apt to be suspect. No one, it seems, objects to growing bigger and better corn and wheat crops by cross-breeding — something that has gone on for centuries. There is no controversy over transplanting the genes from plants that possess nitrogen-processing ability to vegetables that do not, so that they will not require enormous amounts of costly fertilizer, which is as polluting as it is expensive. Or, for that matter, over creating an elm tree that is both beautiful and able to stay free of the deadly fungus infection Dutch elm disease. All of this, and more, might be achieved simply by inserting the right combination of DNA into a plant cell, thereby giving that cell a capability it did not have before. Even now, scientists are working to separate genes that prevent certain fruits from freezing in bad weather. While some fruits manage to survive a severe winter, unfortunately they do not taste very good. If the "antifreeze" genes could be isolated and linked to genes of a tree that bears tasty fruit but is not frost-resistant, something new, plentiful, and delicious would find its way into our supermarkets.

Besides endowing plants with new synthetic capabilities, recombinant DNA research, with its bacteria factories, could be used to produce vast quantities of a new protein or chemical that would do new things, or simply to produce large quantities of others that are either in short supply or not easily obtainable with current methods. One might grow new animals with characteristics they could never acquire in nature — perhaps not a cow that would produce chocolate milk by combining its genes with those from cacao plants, but possibly one that was endowed with the much longer life-span of an Indian elephant, thus enabling it to produce milk for many more years. There may not, of course, be a specific gene that codes for aging, but other beneficial hereditary traits might be fused into an animal that lacked them, thus adding to its other assets.

The potential benefits at this stage are pure speculation, of course. Whether some of the more bizarre projects ever come to pass will depend on what scientists can learn from further experimentation. And therein lies the problem.

There is, as we have said, a growing realization among scientists and laypeople that some of the experiments are dangerous. The results of gene-juggling, they feel, may become more of a curse than a blessing, the same way that the emergence of nuclear energy, powerful new weapons systems, and pesticides are viewed. Experimenting with genes may be even more hazardous than working with nuclear power. New forms of life that might grow out of DNA research, or the emergence of a new disease, might not be as easily contained as atomic energy. As of the moment, thankfully, there has been no instance where a recombinant DNA experiment has created a hazard. This, certainly, does not mean that such a situation will not occur, nor that the fears of concerned individuals — that new germs more deadly than any found naturally could be loosed on the world — are groundless. One justification for this fear arises from the widespread use of *E. coli* bacteria in recombinant DNA experiments. Because it is so common in humans and because it so easily exchanges genetic information with other bacteria, it is a potential biological bomb. Making matters worse is that *E. coli* is also found in every warm-blooded animal, in insects, and in fish. If a new combination of genes produced, let us say, a deadly poison, and this poison were introduced into *E. coli*, it would multiply. The new hybrid could cause a great deal of trouble if it ever escaped from the laboratory and found its way into our sewer systems, where *E. coli* also thrives. Scientists know that some genes are blueprinted to resist drugs such as penicillin, an antibacterial substance produced in certain molds. This happens naturally and is the reason for the relatively common and rapid resistance to important drugs that has been observed over the last twenty or so years. Scientists have learned how to insert those genes into bacteria that ordinarily would be killed by antibiotics. If a technique like that were to get out of hand, there would be more disease against which there would be no defense. Transferring a frost-resistant gene to an orange that does not have one is far different from sending an antibiotic-resistant gene into a deadly germ. Even the transfer of a gene with potential for good could prove harmful. Suppose, for instance, that one could make gallons of insulin by isolating the gene that makes it and growing it in a common bacterium like

E. coli. This would be of enormous benefit to diabetics who require the hormone to control their disease. But what if some of these insulin-producing bacteria escaped and infected large numbers of individuals who do not require insulin?

There is also the possibility that when foreign DNA is inserted into a bacterial gene, it might alter the cell in which it newly found itself, in ways that scientists do not yet know about. Furthermore, when a cell containing recombinant DNA died, it might transfer that fused DNA to the cell of another organism with which it was in contact. If the recombinant DNA got into a cell that was not part of the original experiment, all sorts of unexpected consequences might result from this second recombination.

In 1976 the National Cancer Institute warned against repeating an experiment involving a combination of two viruses unless extreme caution were exercised. The experiment, performed at the Southwest Foundation for Research and Education in San Antonio, Texas, used a virus native to baboons and one capable of causing cancer in mice. The two different viruses were mixed in a laboratory culture dish to produce what is known as a pseudotype virus. When this new virus was injected into beagle puppies, monkeys, and chimpanzees, it caused cancer to grow in those animals. What prompted the warning was that neither of the two viruses — that is, before they were joined — was known to cause cancer in any of the animals that developed the disease after receiving the combination virus. Also, human cells infected with the pseudotype virus in a test tube underwent cancerous changes. According to an official of the Cancer Institute, the new virus was probably the first pseudotype to cause cancer in a higher primate, the chimpanzee, which bears a close genetic resemblance to humans.

It is this sort of experiment — along with one called "shotgunning," in which DNA from a number of unknown genes is put into a bacterium with uncertain results — that has given many scientists reason to pause. They want to know, and rightly, what good would come from the freakish forms that could arise. They ask: Is the natural curiosity of science to be satisfied at all costs, including the possible creation of a "Doomsday Bug"? Does science have the right to alter millions of years of evolution, a natural process that works in its slow way to balance life forms and preserve efficiency?

A situation that developed in Cambridge, Massachusetts, in the summer of 1976 highlights the recombinant DNA controversy. Harvard University, located in the city, had planned to build a new five-hundred-thousand-dollar laboratory where recombinant DNA experiments would be performed. Several concerned scientists, among them Dr. George Wald of Harvard, a Nobel Prize–winning biologist, urged the Cambridge City Council to block construction of the laboratory. Public hearings were held, and the mayor of the city, Alfred E. Vellucci, declared, "We want to be damned sure the people of Cambridge won't be affected by anything that could crawl out of that laboratory. It is my responsibility to investigate the danger of infections to humans. They may come up with a disease that can't be cured, even a monster. Is this the answer to Dr. Frankenstein's dream?"

Scientists lined up on both sides of the issue, and a mock laboratory was even set up during a street fair to present the two viewpoints to the public. Inviting the citizens to come see and hear the pros and cons of DNA research, Mayor Vellucci said: "If elected officials can be carefully scrutinized, so can the scientists. The day of reckoning is fast approaching. There will be no more underhanded or back-room biological shenanigans taking place in our city. Enough is enough."

Scientists who favored a go-ahead on the laboratory suggested that the danger was a possibility, but improbable, and they warned that without the facility many scientists would leave the university and the area and go to other universities to pursue such experiments without undue restriction. Money to support research is generally in short supply, others suggested, and it too would flow elsewhere — to more hospitable laboratories. The Cambridge City Council finally declared a moratorium, a temporary ban, on all recombinant DNA research. The ban was not without precedent. Two years earlier, a committee of prominent American scientists — acting with the approval of the prestigious National Academy of Sciences–National Research Council — also called for a temporary halt to potentially dangerous genetic experiments. Because of the committee's action, many scientists all over the world stopped their DNA research until the experiments could be evaluated for safety, and until some sort of federal guidelines for researchers to follow could be written.

After months of debate, the National Institutes of Health issued guidelines covering potentially dangerous DNA research. Among other things, these policies banned the transplanting of genes that produce poisons into common and harmless bacteria, and experiments that could make deadly germs resistant to drugs now used against them. The guidelines also specified that other potentially dangerous experiments must be performed on weak organisms, so that if any did manage to escape they would not be able to survive in the outside world for very long. Finally, the guidelines said that experiments must be done in special laboratories — so-called clean rooms

— with double doors and a ventilation system that would filter all air that left the lab. These policies are flexible enough to be revised if necessary, in the light of new knowledge that might result from the research.

Most scientists have welcomed the NIH guidelines as necessary to control the revolutionary research work in genetics and cut the chances of unleashing something terrible on the public. Some, however, feel they are not strong enough, that the precautions are not foolproof. Finally, there is fear that while some scientists will now think twice before recombining DNA, others may not. Human nature and scientific curiosity are powerful influences in a laboratory, as is the competition to be first with a new research result. Furthermore, since the guidelines are not laws, there is nothing to prevent biochemists from carrying on recombinant DNA experiments in small laboratories without government funding, or without anyone knowing what they are up to. The research is also done in other countries, all of which have scientists as skilled as our own. Although several nations are trying to regulate such research, there is thus far nothing to compel them to. With so many laboratories working in genetics, it is almost impossible to control and contain all of the organisms involved.

On the other hand, many scientists feel that the guidelines are too strong, too restrictive. As Dr. Donald D. Brown, director of the Carnegie Institution of Laboratories in Baltimore, has put it: "These guidelines are extraordinarily strict, compared to the relatively lax ways other areas of biomedical research known to be fiercely hazardous are handled. It's a clear case of overkill. They are designed to contain molecules in laboratories run by people who have no intention of letting them loose anyway. There is no mass or commercial application for the work. We're not growing test tube babies, and the notion that this work could result in unknown monsters or an 'Andromeda Strain' epidemic is totally unfounded." (In the novel and movie *The Andromeda Strain*, by Michael Crichton, a deadly virus unknown on earth is brought here accidentally in a space capsule. Scientists are unable to deal with the alien organism until they finally analyze it.) Dr. Brown also believes that several problems could be solved instantly with recombinant DNA studies, all of which have no application in genetic engineering. "Frankensteinian spectres raised by proponents of restriction are mostly emotional, political, rhetorical and unscientific," he says. Dr. Brown is not in favor of unbridled research on anything a researcher chooses. Instead of the NIH guidelines, which he sees as inflexible, he has proposed establishment of an objective board of scientists and laypeople, who would look at each research project, evaluate it on its own merits, and find ways for researchers to pursue each project safely. Other critics of the guidelines maintain that recombination of DNA between unrelated species goes on all the time in nature, as, for example, in the intestines of animals. "When mammals die," one scientist explains, "their bodies decompose and their DNA mixes with bacteria. I can't prove it, but I believe that any recombination that we could produce has already occurred over and over again in nature." Natural environments do provide numerous opportunities for mixing DNA, but whether the recombinations always occur and how often is still a mystery.

Lastly, there is the argument that guidelines that might lead to rules and regulations represent a threat to the researcher's freedom. The right to investigate, to seek a scientific truth, is important to every scientist. Too much regulation, it is argued, will eventually destroy scientific freedom and create new Dark Ages of intellectual emptiness.

So the debate goes on. What is clear is that biology or chemistry, as interpreted and applied by imaginative and skilled scientists, has already shaped our lives in ways that our ancestors could hardly have imagined. Whether the good has outweighed the bad in what science has done is still open to discussion. It is also clear that we are now part of another biological and chemical age, a revolution that sooner or later is bound to affect us all as directly as it now affects the seemingly insignificant viruses and bacteria and their tiny specks of DNA. The risks for humanity in what scientists are now able to do are unquestionably greater than they were a century ago. Let us hope that a century from now those risks will be seen to have been worth the taking.

9

Engineering
the Mind

Combining, manufacturing, and manipulating genes are not the only methods scientists use to reshape living systems. One important related technique that we have not yet discussed is mind modification. This could mean improving the brain's function by raising intelligence or sharpening memory. It may also come to mean altering our moods, calming the distraught, or putting the jumbled thought processes of the mentally ill individual in order. However, in a more ominous sense, it may mean the deliberate wiping out of intelligence, erasing memory for questionable motives, or altering beliefs that a government or demagogue might find threatening.

Mind modification can be accomplished with drugs or surgery, or by electrical stimulation of the brain. And it is this area of human engineering that conjures up some of the most frightening images — vague-eyed people doing what a computer or a chemical additive forces them to do. That negative view is due partly to the mystique that surrounds the brain itself, and partly to the chilling exaggerations of behavior therapy that have appeared in novels and movies. We have all read about patients subjected to electric shock or psychosurgery that leaves them docile robots, ready to act on a command from a cruel master, like so many trained dogs. While much of this is overstated to hold the interest of the intended audience, mind control *is* a reality, and some of the techniques employed by science are not too far removed from the world of science fiction. But before one can consider how scientists control the brain, it's necessary to understand something about how it works.

The brain, as everyone knows, is a lump of wrinkled gray matter sitting in virtual isolation in our skulls. It controls the nervous system, that delicate and complicated network that sends its branches into every part of the body. In one way or another, it is in charge of everything we do. Synonymous with mind, intelligence, judgment, memory, learning, and creativity, the brain is a master computer, an electrical instrument that is at work every time we love, hate, fear, desire, hunger, and thirst. It is the single organ vital to behavior, be it violent or peaceful. Since it is linked by nerves to all parts of the body, it is in command of other actions. Every time we feel, smell, hear, move, speak, and see, its messages — electrical charges created by chemical action — pulse throughout our bodies.

The brain's communication system is made up of billions of nerve cells called neurons, each having a special job. These cells far outnumber the total of all of the transistors in all of the world's computers. Tiny nerve branches connect the cells to each other and to the spinal cord, over which the electrochemical messages are transmitted and received. Each person has his or her own distinctive brain-wave pattern, the result of this electrical current discharge. All of this electrical activity may be traced by a technique called electroencephalography, in which tiny wires are attached to the scalp and connected to a vacuum-tube amplifier. There they are magnified more than a million times and made to activate an electromagnetic pen that writes the encephalogram, or EEG, on a moving strip of paper. The EEG is used to determine, among other states, the death of an individual: when the brain wave expresses itself as a flat line for a certain length of time, for instance, the brain cells are considered to be dead.

Electrical activity in animals — and not only in their brains — has been known for thousands of years. Aristotle, three hundred years before Christ, was aware of the phenomenon, but he did not call it electricity. In his *History of Animals,* the philosopher wrote: "The torpedo fish narcotizes the creatures it wants to catch, overpowering them by the strength of shock that is resident in its body, and feeds upon them. It is known to cause a numbness even in human beings."

An interesting account of bioelectricity has been written by Dr. E. E. Suckling, a physics professor at Downstate Medical Center, State University of New York, Brooklyn. Published under the auspices of the American Institute of Biological Sciences, Dr. Suckling's monograph notes that it was not until 1774 that John Walsh, a fellow of the British Royal Society, wrote to Benjamin Franklin (who had conducted his lightning experiments twelve years earlier) to say that ". . . the effect of the torpedo fish appears to be absolutely electrical . . . the back and breast of the animal are in different states of electricity." This was the first time anyone had strongly suggested that an animal had electric-shock power. In the book *Cyborg:*

Evolution of the Superman, author D. S. Halacy, Jr., takes that a step further, discussing some applications of such biopower: "Fifty years ago, a biologist named Potter put together a number of yeast 'cells' to make a biobattery with an output of a tiny fraction of a watt. He discovered that his living cells had a voltage of about half a volt. For half a century, this remained an interesting laboratory curiosity. Then in the late 1950s, a number of researchers picked up the ball and began to run in all directions. As a result, the Navy developed 'marine biocells' in which microorganisms obligingly converted marine matter into modest amounts of electricity to power small pieces of electronic equipment needed on buoys and other floating gear.

"Another group demonstrated a radio powered by a test tube full of seawater and bacteria, and operated a model boat on a similar biocell taking its fuel from the water. There was the standard amount of loose talk of converting the Black Sea into a huge biobattery to bring a kind of TVA [Tennessee Valley Authority, a system of hydroelectric plants that provides cheap power] to underprivileged Asiatics who had never before known the blessings of electric power." (*Cyborg*, incidentally, is a coined word that means "man plus machine." Cybernetics is the study of the control processes in physical and biological systems.)

One well-known bioelectric phenomenon occurs in our hearts. In every mammal, that organ contains a region of specialized muscle tissue, near the point where the great blood vessels enter, where the energy that triggers the heartbeat originates. The region is called a pacemaker, and the stimulus found there is electrical. Like other electrical events that occur in living creatures, this stimulus is not fully understood. But now physicians can place battery-powered pacemakers in individuals whose heart rhythm is faulty. Small enough to be implanted under the skin, these electrical devices supply the pulses that command the heart to beat properly. There are some 250,000 electric pacemakers in use in the United States, most of which are operated by batteries that last up to six years. Because of their relatively short life-span, the pacemakers must be removed periodically to have their power supplies replenished. Another kind of electrical device is the nerve pacemaker, which is implanted in a patient's back to relieve pain. This works by using low-voltage electrical waves to block the nerve messages of pain that are transmitted over the spinal cord.

Electricity has also been used to put goldfish to sleep — by running a current through their tanks — and to produce sleep in humans who are to undergo surgery. A pioneer in this field of electrical stimulation is Dr. José M. R. Delgado, professor of physiology at Yale University. In 1954 Dr. Delgado performed experiments in which he electrically stimulated the brains of cats, rats, and monkeys. By doing so, he was able to control psychological phenomena in the animals. He stimulated or inhibited learning, pain, and pleasure with the use of electric charges. Later, by stimulating the brains of human patients, he was able to soothe the violent, relieve pain, and influence such mental functions as the thinking process, speech, and memory. Dr. Delgado's most sensational attempt to control aggressive animal behavior came in a bull ring. Planting himself directly in the path of a charging bull that had electrodes implanted in its brain, Dr. Delgado stopped the animal in its tracks via radio signals. In 1970 he and his team established, for the first time, direct, two-way radio communication between an animal's brain and a computer. The experiment was performed on a six-year-old chimp named Paddy, who was placed on an artificial island that simulated natural conditions as nearly as possible. Electrodes implanted in Paddy's brain picked up electrical waves and sent them to a computer. The computer, programmed to recognize particular patterns of electrical impulses, then returned a control signal to another part of Paddy's brain. What it all meant was that a method had been devised by which the brain — without the direct help of any of the senses — signals itself in order to control a particular function. What Dr. Delgado did, in effect, was talk directly to the brain.

Dr. Delgado's work has, of course, promoted the same arguments about control for evil purposes that swirl about genetic engineers. The scientist believes, however, that his experiments have very important implications for the treatment of human brain disorders, particularly diseases known to be caused by electrical disturbances in the brain. One application might involve treating patients with epilepsy, a chronic disorder marked by abnormal brain-wave function. Epileptics sometimes suffer convulsions, and some erupt in violent rage due, it has been shown, to the erratic patterns of electrical brain waves — known as "electrical storms." An outgrowth of Dr. Delgado's work might be a miniature brain pacemaker that could be implanted in the epileptic's body to receive and send electrical information. With such a pacemaker, an epileptic would have important areas of his or her brain's electrical activity monitored by a remote computer. Electrical disturbances that might lead to convulsive attacks would be detected and corrected by the computer, while the patient continued normal activities, uninterrupted by the now blocked attack. "Many such difficult cases of epilepsy, pain, motor abnormalities, and perhaps even mental illness may be treatable by this combination of neurophysiological technology, microsurgery and electronics," Dr. Delgado has said. "Patients would benefit from the on-demand, precise application of radio instructions to the limited areas of their brains responsible for their diseases, and may be free to live more normal lives without medication or suffering." Dr. Delgado cautions, however, that the possibility of establishing direct communication between brain and computer, without the intervention of the senses or the conscious knowledge of the subject, presents "new and increasingly complex philosophical problems about the future of man."

There are many other examples, apart from those involving Dr. Delgado's experiments, of the use of electrical stimulation of the brain to alter behavior or a medical condition. At Tulane University, Dr. Robert G. Heath has implanted more than a hundred electrodes at a time into the brains of patients suffering from a wide range of mental problems and pains. By electrically stimulating one of the brain's regions, he brought about feelings of pleasure and was also able to wipe out pain. Dr. Heath has also suggested that by controlling pleasure one can alter patterns of learned behavior — for example, in some homosexual subjects, he has successfully changed the repellent feelings they had toward the opposite sex into pleasurable ones. In another application of biopower, a team of California scientists a few years ago devised an experimental artificial brain for overcoming paralysis due to stroke. Stroke, the third most common cause of death in the United States, occurs when there is interference with the blood supply to the brain. The blocking of an artery in the brain by a clot, or thrombus, can bring on a stroke, as can the bursting of a brain artery, an event that floods the surrounding tissue with blood. Whatever the cause, during a stroke the blood supply to part of the brain is cut off, and the nerve cells in that portion quit functioning. As a result, parts of the body controlled by the paralyzed nerve cells cannot function. The stroke victim may have difficulty walking, speaking, or remembering, and there may be paralysis in an arm, leg, or the face. The California scientists, working at the Stanford Research Institute and Stanford University School of Medicine, used their artificial brain on monkeys to produce a number of movements in an otherwise paralyzed limb. The device consisted of an array of electrodes implanted in several key sites of the brain. These were linked to an external computer, which was programmed to stimulate them electrically so as to evoke a coordinated range of arm and leg movements. (Strokes had been produced in the monkeys by artificially putting out of commission certain areas of the brain that control limb function.) According to the scientists, computer programs were written that stimulated the electrodes in precise sequence, so as to produce various movements in the animals, including: making a paralyzed limb reach out, grasp an object, such as food, and bring the object rapidly and smoothly to the animal's mouth; extending a limb outward and upward, as in climbing; extending an arm backward over the body with a back-and-forth movement, as in scratching. The team reported in the journal *Stroke* that, with a little training, the animal could be given a set of switches that tell the computer what set of movements to produce in the paralyzed limb(s). In this way, the monkey could control his own behavior according to need. The researchers believe that the technique might be extended to many other forms of deficiency due to brain injury or disease, including coma, mental retardation, and some forms of blindness. With regard to loss of sight, the idea of an artificial-vision device using electrodes implanted in the skull is not a particularly new one. Electrical stimulation of the visual-control area of the brain was applied as far back as 1953. Some years later, Drs. Giles S. Brindley and W. S. Lewin of the University of Cambridge in England implanted eighty electrodes inside the skull of a fifty-two-year-old woman who had become blind; they connected them to a series of miniature radio receivers implanted in the scalp. Some of the electrodes, as the researchers and the woman were pleased to note, stimulated tiny, flickering spots of light before her eyes. More recently, an article in the journal *Science* reported on the work of teams from the University of Utah's Institute for Biomedical Engineering, and the University of Western Ontario. Two young men, volunteers in the study, had been blind for seven and twenty-eight years respectively; but when they were "plugged" into a computer with sixty-four tiny platinum electrode points stimulating the surfaces of their brains, they saw distinct points of light. They said also they were able to recognize simple patterns, including some letters, and draw on paper what they saw. Heartening as the results of the experiment were, and despite the fact that the general technology exists to construct an artificial-vision device, much work remains to be done before such equipment can truly benefit patients. The ultimate goal of such work would be the perfection of a system allowing the blind to perceive images, through a camera mounted in a glass eye and connected to electrodes stimulating the visual area of the brain. Prototypes are expected to be developed over the next few years in the University of Utah's labs, according to William H. Dobelle, the project director. Researchers say the glass eye containing a miniaturized camera would be attached to the patient's eye muscles. The various levels of light sensed by the camera would then be transmitted to a subminiature digital computer, built into the frames of dummy glasses. Resulting images, the scientists believe, would depend on the number of electrodes implanted. They could range from the simple outline of an obstacle in the blind person's path to something as complex as the outline of a human face. It is also hoped that the device will permit reading ordinary printed material at useful speeds. Experiments to date have involved only a few moments of electrical stimulation, which is a safe amount. Much more, however, needs to be learned from animal studies about the effects of continuous electrical stimulation for years, let alone days.

One of the most controversial uses of electrical stimulation is electric shock treatment, also called electroconvulsive therapy, or ECT. Misunderstood by many people, shock treatments are often used to treat depression. Contrary to popular opinion, ECT is not a discredited procedure, and though it has its detractors, it is a relatively safe treatment. The American Psychiatric Association, in fact, has issued statements saying that shock is highly effective in treating moderate and severe depression, and can often end the problem in a matter of days, virtually always within a month. A wide variety of antidepressant drugs are also available, but their effectiveness is variable and response to them may take longer and be less predictable than shock. Shock therapy is not, of course, a cure for any disorder. It can, however, put an end to an episode of depression, giving a psychiatrist time to get at the root of the problem. While no one really knows why the passage of a current of electricity through the brain wipes away depression, chances are that it alters the brain's chemistry, and thereby the emotions. Shock may also stimulate or change the "setting" of the hypothalamus, the supreme master of the body's brain-hormone system. Situated in front of the brain stem, the hypothalamus is packed with nerve centers that monitor and regulate body temperature and blood pressure, and regulate sexual activity, hunger, thirst, water balance, digestion, and the wake-sleep cycle. When experimentally stimulated with electricity, the hypothalamus produces a broad range of sensations and emotional reactions in both animals and humans — intense pleasure, terror, rage, and calm. The chemicals it produces activate or prevent the release of various hormones that come from another gland, the pea-sized pituitary, to which it is connected by nerve fibers. These hormones travel through the bloodstream until they reach other endocrine glands, which are stimulated to release their own hormones. These then go on to perform an incredible array of jobs, aimed at regulating the activities of cells and organs and controlling various emotional and bodily functions.

In a standard shock treatment, the patient is given medication to put him or her to sleep, and another to relax the muscles. Then electrodes are taped to the temples and a 110-volt current is passed into the brain. The current is applied for only a few seconds, and ten to twelve treatments are often necessary to cure the depression. Temporary amnesia, or loss of memory, occurs after shock therapy. Some psychiatrists believe this could develop into a permanent memory lapse if too many treatments are administered.

Electric shock is also used in a treatment known as aversion therapy, or conditioned avoidance. In this case, the electric current is tied to some objectionable impulse the patient is trying to get rid of. An alcoholic, for example, may be given a shock each time a drink is set before him or her. Eventually, the alcoholic associates the two and develops an aversion, or dislike, for the liquor. This form of treatment is known generally as behavior therapy, and there is considerable disagreement over whether it provides a permanent cure. Various conditioning and desensitizing techniques are employed by behavior therapists — aversion therapy is only one of them — to help a patient relearn and thus bring about a desired form of behavior. Behavior therapy deemphasizes the unconscious part of a patient and what is in his or her past; it concentrates, instead, on current behavior and problems. Human beings who undergo behavior therapy are treated somewhat like animals who can be trained or taught to rid themselves of undesirable habits. Those of you who read the novel *A Clockwork Orange,* or saw the movie based on it, will recall Alex, the central character. An extremely violent and guiltless person, Alex undergoes conditioning aimed at altering his horrid behavior. He is tied up, and his eyes are propped open. Then he is forced to watch film after film depicting all forms of violence. At last his former behavior becomes sickening to him, and he is changed into a socially well-adjusted person.

A more drastic form of mind control is psychosurgery, a procedure in which tiny portions of brain tissue are destroyed or removed to change a person's emotional makeup, to lessen pain, or to control destructive behavior. Sometimes bits of brain are burned out with special instruments, other times they are simply cut out with a scalpel. Psychosurgery goes by many names — topectomy, cingulectomy, leucotomy, and lobotomy, to name a few. Actually, the practice of opening the human skull to relieve pain and pressure goes back many thousands of years, and there is fossil evidence to show that several primitive peoples did just that. A sharp instrument called a trepan was used to cut holes in the skull, and quite a number of these cutting knives have been dug up. Anthropologists theorize that these early trepanations were performed to release harmful spirits that were blamed for strange behavior or headaches. However, there is also evidence that holes were deliberately cut into skulls that also bore head injuries — proof that these crude surgeons knew enough to remove broken bits of bone pressed into the brain.

Lobotomy does work to alter behavior, but the public has grown increasingly sensitive to the procedure because of the ethical questions that it raises. Physicians too have criticized the operation. One of the most outspoken has been Dr. Peter R. Breggin, a Washington psychiatrist and a member of the Medical Committee for Human Rights. He once told the U.S. Senate Health Subcommittee, chaired by Senator Edward M. Kennedy: "If America ever falls to totalitarianism, the dictator will be a behavioral scientist, and the chief of police will be armed with lobotomy and psychosurgery." Dr. Breggin also charged that brain operations designed to control behavior were being performed, even though they had little demonstrable value, and that they were being done on people with relatively intact personalities, "solely for the purpose of making them less aggressive." He said also that many of the operations were being done on hyperactive children, some only five years old, with neurotic women in their middle years being the largest group undergoing such surgery. Neurosurgeons who perform the operation have responded by saying that it is generally done to alleviate functional brain disorders or when all else — medications and psychotherapy — fails. It is not performed, they reply, to pacify potential radicals, as some have charged.

In July of 1973, the National Association for Mental

Health released a statement on psychosurgery. The statement said that it should not be used except when the patient is in such great emotional stress, due to mental disorder, that he or she, by personal choice, would prefer the operation to living with the existing mental condition. "Because psychosurgery is still, to a large extent, experimental, it is absolutely essential that there be safeguards to protect patients who might otherwise be used as human guinea pigs," said Mrs. J. Skelly Wright, president of the association. The association's position was that psychosurgery be regarded as a last resort, to be considered only when all other alternatives have been given adequate trial in the opinion of the patient, the family, and at least two reputable physicians, one of whom should be a psychiatrist.

We should mention here a technique called biofeedback. While it does not fall into the "brainwashing" category, as some of the techniques discussed in this chapter do, it is nonetheless a way of exerting control over one's body and mind. The controller, however, is *you*. And the person you control is yourself. It works like this: Your body's natural rhythms and internal functions — such things as brain waves, heartbeat, muscle tension, skin temperature, and blood pressure — are picked up by electronic devices and amplified. You might, for instance, "see" your heartbeat inked out on a graph, or "hear" your brain waves as a series of high-pitched beeps. By "watching" and "listening" to such usually unconscious occurrences, a person can influence his or her own physical and mental well-being. In effect you can will your blood pressure to drop, raise your body temperature merely by thinking about it, even control epileptic seizures by learning how to produce the right brain waves. At Boston City Hospital a few years ago, investigators demonstrated how

five out of seven patients were able to reduce their blood
pressure by 9 percent through their conscious reaction to
tones, lights, and projected slides. The patients who par-
ticipated in the experiment were told that they would be
paid five dollars a session to come to the laboratory and
have their blood pressure measured automatically for
about an hour while they sat quietly. No medications
were to be used. During the sessions, the patients sat in
isolation chambers, each of which contained a screen onto
which slides were projected. The slides were of scenic
pictures, and reminders of the money to be earned. A
small microphone was also fixed under the blood-pressure
cuff attached to each patient's arm. This microphone
picked up what are called Korotkoff sounds, which are
produced by the blood flow through the artery when pressure is applied to the cuff. A relatively low blood pressure,
indicated by the absence of the sound, was fed back to the
patients on each heartbeat. This low-blood-pressure reading was indicated simultaneously by a brief flash of light
and a tone of moderate intensity. The researchers told the
patients that the tone and the light were desirable, and
that they ought to make them reappear. As a reward, after
each twenty presentations of tone and light, a photo-
graphic slide worth five cents was shown for five seconds.
At the end of the experiment, there was a marked drop in
the patients' average blood pressure.

Lights or tones have also been used to alert patients to
a particular neurological change in the brain, such as occurs during epileptic seizures. With biofeedback techniques, some patients have been able to reduce their
seizures by achieving some degree of voluntary suppres-
sion of the motor disturbance when they feel it coming
on.

Producing the correct brain waves, according to researchers, may be accompanied by a pleasant, energized state. There may also be a decrease in anxiety and depression. This is not too difficult to understand when you realize that each of our different brain-wave lengths — known as alpha, beta, theta, and delta — is associated with some mental state. During periods of meditation and relaxation, for instance, those who practice Zen and yoga generate alpha waves almost exclusively. Beta waves appear to be released during anxious moments, delta during sleep, and theta in periods of creativity. By listening to these waves, amplified electronically, some people are able to regulate their mental states, relax without the use of medication, improve memory and the powers of concentration, and sleep better. Several hundred scientists are now testing biofeedback techniques because of their great medical potential. Biofeedback could, for example, become an important tool for psychotherapists and physiologists alike — the former using it to teach patients to control their own emotional difficulties, the latter using it to allow individuals to regulate bodily functions, such as their heartbeats or the amount of oxygen they consume.

Another way of altering behavior is through drugs and chemicals. Drugs such as amphetamines (also called "speed"), cocaine, and the caffeine in coffee, tea, chocolate, and cola drinks stimulate the central nervous system; that is, they give us extra energy. Barbiturates, heroin, and alcohol are, on the other hand, central-nervous-system depressants — they slow us down, make us very lazy, and can bring on sleep. People who take cocaine feel as though they can go on forever, talking fast and pacing about; on heroin, users simply lie about lazily in a dreamy state. There are also drugs that distort our perceptions, drugs like LSD and mescaline. There is no doubt, then, that chemicals can turn you on and off, whether they are prescribed by a doctor, taken illicitly at pill parties, or found naturally in the brain, as so many are. An example of the naturally occurring substances was the discovery in 1957, by scientists at Tulane University, of a strange chemical in the blood of schizophrenics. When they injected this chemical, named taraxein, into monkeys, it caused changes in brain waves very much like those found in schizophrenics. Furthermore, when the chemical was given to human volunteers who were not afflicted with the mental illness, they, too, developed schizophrenic behavior.

Brain chemistry may also be a factor in aggressive behavior, just as it is in schizophrenia and mental retardation. For instance, the male hormone can increase feelings of aggressiveness in those adolescents who generally feel inferior. A number of drugs, as we have said, can elevate one's mood, and others can cause depression. These mood swings appear to be linked in some way to key brain chemicals called biogenic amines, and many scientists are convinced that drugs that affect our emotional state do so by altering these chemicals. The amines are made in the body from amino acids, the natural substances that also make protein. How drugs interact with brain chemicals to alter mood is not well understood, but it is known that mood-elevating drugs tend to speed up the activity of some amines, while mood-depressing drugs slow them down. It is still too early to say, however, that the amines are definitely involved in violent behavior, or in mental disorders that can cause such behavior.

Nevertheless several experiments have shown that brain chemicals can and do induce violent action, in both animals and human beings. In 1970 a dramatic experiment that lent strong support to this idea was performed at Princeton University. Twelve rats that normally never killed mice were injected with a drug, carbachol, in the brain area responsible for emotion. The drug imitates the action of a chemical that occurs naturally in the brain, and is believed to be related to the transmission of nerve impulses. Astonishingly, every one of the injected rats killed mice placed in their cages. It was also interesting to note that each drug-induced killing had the same appearance as a natural killing — that is, the mouse was killed with a bite through the cervical spinal cord — even though the rats had never killed before nor seen other rats kill. When the scientists reversed the process — that is, injected a substance that blocked the action of the brain chemical mimicked by carbachol — the killer rats merely sniffed at mice placed in their cages and did not attack them. An experiment like this raises the possibility that drugs may one day be used to treat human aggressors. A few years ago, in fact, the president of the American Psychological Association, Dr. Kenneth B. Clark, suggested that new drugs be created to eliminate inhumanity. These drugs, he said, could be given routinely to national leaders to hold down their hostile and aggressive impulses and allow more reasoned, humane behavior to take over. A powerful leader who took such a drug, for instance, might not ever consider initiating a nuclear war, or unleashing potent biological weapons to spread disease over a population. Dr. Clark also suggested that such "psychological disarmament" might be used on the general population to strengthen people's sense of morality and justice. However, Dr. Clark added that he was quite aware that the use of such mind-altering drugs posed considerable difficulty, and that he did not believe in creating a society of friendly human robots. "[We] must not destroy the creative, evaluative and selective capacities of human beings," he emphasized. "Without the desire to explore, to reorganize things and ideas, to vary moods and to produce, the human being would be an empty organic vessel and it would be difficult to justify the mere fact of survival under these conditions."

Researchers, of course, are interested not only in controlling violent and aggressive behavior when they manipulate brain chemicals. The correction of brain disorders and afflictions may also result from work with neurotransmitters, the chemicals that control mood and thought. Consider, for a moment, Parkinson's disease, a nervous disorder. Also called shaking palsy, the disease causes stiffness of the muscles, trembling, stooped posture, masklike rigidity of the face, and difficulty in walking, writing, and speaking. It generally attacks people in their fifties and sixties, and though it is rarely a primary cause of death, it often so weakens the victim that he or she develops other diseases. The cause of Parkinson's disease is unknown, but a strong theory is that it is brought on by a brain chemical out of control. Muscle coordination, goes the theory, depends on a delicate balance of two neurochemical systems called cholinergic and dopaminergic. The symptoms of Parkinsonism may stem from overactivity or underactivity of one or the other of these systems. The theory has been strengthened by recent progress in drug treatment that is believed to work by correcting these chemical imbalances. Recent research has centered on a chemical called dopamine, found naturally in the brain. Essential to nerve-impulse transmission, it has been found in short supply in patients with Parkinsonism. The drug L-dopa is currently used to correct the chemical imbalance and thus help victims of the disease. In somewhat the same fashion, the drug lithium is used to correct imbalances of another neurotransmitter, serotonin, in the treatment of manic-depression, a mental disorder characterized by dramatic swings of mood between high and low.

Another disorder in which brain chemicals are apparently at work is hyperkinesis, a complicated medical problem linked to serious learning difficulties in children. Young persons afflicted with the problem are unable to concentrate, have poor memory, do not listen or coordinate their eyes and hands well, and are unable to sit still. According to one leading specialist in the disorder, Dr. Eric Denhoff, a clinical associate professor of pediatrics at Brown University, the general symptoms of hyperkinesis — a word with Greek roots that means "excessive movement" — arise from a medical, not a psychological, problem. The disorder occurs, he explains, when a child's brain lacks enough of two key central-nervous-system chemicals, noradrenalin and dopamine. These are necessary for the transmission of information from one part of the brain to another.

"Mankind," says Dr. Denhoff, "actually has three brains in one" — a middle brain that controls behavior; the cortex, which restrains or controls thought processes; and the brain stem, which controls the functions necessary for life, such as heart rate and breathing. "When in certain youngsters there is either damage to the brain, which is uncommon, or poor connections between the middle brain and the cortex, stress leads to a situation in which these children have too little noradrenalin to keep the middle brain and the cortex in balance," the doctor says. Stress is the key factor that promotes the chemical imbalance, and that is why anxiety, often produced by school, can bring out the overenergetic "go-go-go" behavior.

Up to 20 percent of all hyperactive children can be aided by medication, Denhoff believes. Through the use of various drugs, additional noradrenalin is made available in a child's nervous system to give the brain cells the ability to transmit information in an orderly way. When a balance is established within the three areas of the brain, hyperactivity lessens, or it is eliminated altogether.

The Brown researcher has completed studies demonstrating the learning-enhancing ability of these drugs with children suffering the brain problem. Before medication, such children had a good deal of difficulty memorizing. But after taking a noradrenalin stimulant, their ability was greatly improved. Similar improvements were measured for other learning tasks. Thus, says Dr. Denhoff, while drugs are not a cure-all for hyperkinetic children, they do help a great number of such children. Some 20 to 30 percent of all hyperactive youngsters continue to carry the disease into adult life, the doctor says. They then become candidates for psychiatric treatment, even though they are really suffering from an undiagnosed physical ailment.

If drugs can enhance learning and memory in children with disorders like hyperkinesis, what is the possibility of finding a drug to markedly improve intelligence in normal individuals? Or of discovering some way to actually transfer learning from one person to another? It would be nice to be able to store up a huge supply of knowledge without having to study, maybe not ever even having to open a book. Unfortunately, nothing in a bottle can yet give us algebra; nor can we now receive an "intelligence transfusion" while lying in a comfortable hospital bed, next to the brilliant person who has agreed to donate some brain chemicals or brain cells. Scientists, however, are working on it, and a number of experts have demonstrated that chemicals can improve and transfer learning, if not in humans, at least in some other living organisms. Scientists have also discovered that certain brain proteins are responsible for storing long-term memory. In experiments with goldfish at McLean Hospital in Belmont, Massachusetts, Dr. Victor Shashoua recently identified three specific natural brain proteins that are needed by the brain to fix information. Moreover, these proteins are produced only in one part of the brain. The finding of this "brain center" for the proteins came as a surprise because most scientists had assumed that long-term memory storage was a function of all brain cells. Interesting to note, the part of the brain in which the special proteins are produced is destroyed in alcoholics who, it is well known, suffer from long-term memory loss. Scientists still don't know exactly how the proteins are used to store information, but once they do, they will have an important clue to the treatment of diseases such as senility, which is the loss of mental faculties associated with old age.

Getting back to drugs that improve learning, the first report of such a substance was in 1918. Karl S. Lashley, an American psychologist who performed a number of important experiments on the learning processes of rats, used strychnine, a stimulant-poison that is deadly in humans, to improve the learning ability of his laboratory animals. Later, scientists found that other stimulant drugs, such as amphetamines, enhanced learning in mice injected with them. Monkeys too have responded well to certain stimulants, learning to perform certain tasks better after an injection. Whether the stimulants will work the same way in humans has yet to be determined. The drugs used to improve learning in animals are potent ones, and they could upset the human brain's chemical balance in such a way that more harm than good might result. Some scientists have pointed out, for instance, that even a single injection of "speed" can upset a human being's pattern of sleep for months at a time. Then, of course, there is the matter of testing the drugs in retarded individuals — a group in which any improvement in learning could be rather easily measured. What of their rights if someone decides to use them as human guinea pigs? It is one thing for a person who is capable of consenting to such an experiment, but quite another for a subject who is not. There is something else to be considered. If drugs can be found to improve intelligence, it should also be possible to come up with drugs to lower it, or to erase memory. Goldfish, for example, that have been taught to swim to certain parts of an aquarium can have that learning ability wiped out by an injection of a particular antibiotic that prevents the formation of brain protein.

Memory transfer, possibly by injecting a brain substance from one animal or human into another, has also intrigued scientists. Like much of the speculation mentioned in this book, the idea is not new. In his story of *Gulliver's Travels*, Jonathan Swift describes a "cephalic tincture" ink that could be used to transfer learning from the stomach up to the brain:

> I was at a mathematical school, where the master taught his pupils after a method scarce imaginable to us in Europe. The proposition and demonstration were fairly written on a thin wafer, with ink composed of a cephalic tincture. This the student was allowed to swallow upon a fasting stomach, and for three days following eat nothing but bread and water. As the wafer digested, the tincture mounted to his brain, bearing the proposition along with it. But the success has not hitherto been answerable, partly by some error in the quantum or composition, and partly by the perverseness of lads, to whom this bolus [rounded mass] is so nauseous, that they generally

steal aside, and discharge it upwards before it can operate; neither have they been yet persuaded to use so long an abstinence as the prescription requires.

On a more scientific note, back in 1962 Dr. James V. McConnell of the University of Michigan performed a fascinating experiment in learning transfer. First, he trained flatworms to react in a certain way to light. (Worms have a number of sensory receptors in their bodies, along with "eye spots" and a large ganglion, or brain.) Then, Dr. McConnell chopped up the trained worms and fed the pieces to untrained worms. Tested after the cannibalistic meal, the second group of worms was found to have picked up a receptivity to the response to light that the trained worms had. Though they still had to be trained to learn the response, they learned faster than the first group of worms did. Similar experiments have been done with rats and mice. In one, brain chemicals were extracted from rats that had been trained to make their way through a maze; when the chemicals were injected into the brains of untrained rats, the animals ran through the maze faster than rats that had not received the chemicals. The scientist who did the experiment, Dr. Georges Ungar of the Texas Medical Center, has also demonstrated that a learned fear of the dark can also be transferred from one rat to another. By giving a rat an electric shock every time it tried to enter a dark hole, Dr. Ungar conditioned it to be afraid. Later, chemicals were removed from the rat's brain and the research team isolated what they believed to be *the* chemical responsible for the animal's attitude toward the dark. They then broke it down in the laboratory, and made a copy of it in a test tube. Injected into normal rats who always try to hide in a dark place, the artificial-memory chemical made them behave in the same way that the conditioned rat had — they refused to enter dark holes. Dr. Ungar and his colleagues have named that brain chemical scotophobin, after the Greek for "fear of the dark." Since their original work, the Texas scientists have isolated other chemicals that appear to transfer learned behavior. Two of these, extracted from goldfish brains, make the fish avoid the colors green and blue; two others, from rat brains, bring on a tolerance to morphine, and enable the animal to become accustomed to sound stimuli. When each of these chemicals is injected into untrained animals, they appear to transfer the behavior they produce. No one seems to know exactly how these memory chemicals are made in the brain, or how the coded information they contain is actually transferred. Messenger and transfer RNA may be at work here, just as they are when a specific protein is to be assembled.

Finally, let's examine how the brain is affected by nutritional inadequacies. These have an adverse effect on the central nervous system, and studies have shown that learning and behavior are affected. Furthermore, the retardation that is caused by an inadequate diet may be permanent and irreversible, no matter how adequate the diet later on. Even more disturbing is that sluggish brain development may be carried over from generation to generation.

A lack of protein in the diet particularly affects the brain. While a baby is in the womb, it receives the vital amino acids its brain cells need for growth from the protein the mother eats. After birth, the infant gets its aminos from mother's milk and from other foods. If the supply of aminos is cut down while the mother is carrying the child or just after its birth, brain growth is stunted and learning slows down. Scientists have done a number of experiments to prove this. When they deprived pregnant rats of protein, for example, they found that their offspring had fewer brain cells. Also, when they fed animals low-protein diets, the levels of key enzymes and amino acids dropped. At Cornell University, experimenters noted that when they fed pigs a low-protein diet for two months after weaning, they grew up as slow learners and were easily upset.

As interesting as these animal experiments are, however, the results that scientists get from them are not always easily applicable to humans. It is, as we have suggested elsewhere, morally unacceptable to perform some experiments on humans, and few researchers would want, or be allowed, to deliberately withhold nourishing proteins from infants. Animal protein studies, therefore, are extremely important and tell us much, more so when the results are compared to field observations of humans who live in a poor environment, in an underdeveloped country, for instance, where nutritious food is in short supply. Thus researchers have been able to conclude that adults who suffered malnutrition during early childhood usually have a lower level of intellectual performance than men and women raised in a similar environment but with an adquate diet. Children who are malnourished may also have a lack of drive and may do poorly on psychological tests, with lower than normal IQs.

Some scientists, however, believe that early malnutrition may only delay brain development, rather than do irreversible damage. One who feels that way is Ana G. Colmenares of Boston University School of Medicine. While she was a graduate student in anatomy at the school, she reported on experiments in which she reversed the effects of a near-starvation diet on the brains of baby rats by giving them a normal diet. In her study, rats fed a low-protein diet from the middle of gestation (pregnancy) until they were twenty days old had significantly smaller brains than rats fed a normal diet. When the malnourished animals were placed on a normal diet, their brains were found to have grown to normal size by seventy days of age; the brains appeared to be no different from the brains of rats that had never been malnourished. The young scientist feels that a new concept may be emerging that holds that even though early malnutrition does lead to retarded brain development, this effect can be reversed if proper nutrition is begun soon enough. Colmenares points out that more work is needed to explore such questions as how low the protein content of the diet can be and how long the malnutrition can be imposed before delayed brain growth becomes irreversible. At the same time she says her findings appear to confirm the results of some recent studies on humans, suggesting that normal intellectual function is possible if malnutrition early in life — that is, during the first two years — is subsequently reversed. In one of these studies, a group of Korean children brought to the United States to be adopted were examined on arrival and found to be severely malnourished. Several years later, when they had started school, they were found to be performing normally for their age.

Promoting intelligence by giving someone a good diet does not, of course, raise any of the urgent moral, social, and legal issues that are posed by the other, more drastic, forms of behavior control and modification we have been discussing — a palatable, optimistic note on which to end this chapter.

10
Conclusion

At the beginning of this book a crucial question was asked: If we are ever able to do some of the things mentioned here, should we do them? It should be obvious by now that the question is not easily answered.

There is another query that you should ponder at this point: Do right ends justify any means? In Shakespeare's *Merchant of Venice*, Bassanio answers the question in the affirmative when he offers to pay Shylock in cash rather than in Antonio's agreed-upon pound of flesh: "And, I beseech you / Wrest once the law to your authority: To do a great right, do a little wrong, / And curb this cruel devil of his will."

Although the second question has not been asked directly in the pages you have just read, it is implied in much of what has been said. You can ask it along with the first one when considering recombinant DNA research, test-tube babies, Dr. Delgado's behavior-control methods, or the use of a live virus to carry a necessary enzyme into a child with a genetic disorder. Ask these questions when considering Dr. Kenneth Clark's suggestion that drugs be used to curb hostility. Or when you discuss psycho-surgery.

Let's consider for a moment some of the suggestions of a prominent Harvard psychologist, B. F. Skinner. Professor Skinner has contributed a great deal to what has come to be known as the technology of behavior. His inventions include the Skinner box, a mechanism for measuring and observing changes in animal behavior; the Air Crib, a mechanical baby tender in which his second daughter spent most of the first thirty months of her life; and the so-called Teaching Machine. In 1959 it was revealed that during World War II Skinner had even trained pigeons to pilot bombs and torpedoes, although the war ended before the pigeons' skills were used. His methods have been used to get prisoners to work toward their rehabilitation and to teach the mentally retarded to behave in ways that are socially acceptable.

A few years ago, Skinner expressed the provocative view that man must surrender the basic rights of life, liberty, and the pursuit of happiness if culture is to survive. "What we need," he observed in his book *Beyond Freedom and Dignity*, "is more control, not less." In exerting more control over the individual, he believes, society should design checks on his or her behavior, so that wrong actions likely to be punished would not occur. In Skinner's opinion, man as we have known him — with his claims to individual freedom and dignity — is nearing extinction. Society has failed man badly by permitting him too much of the wrong kind of freedom. The hostility and aggression shown by many of America's youth, Skinner says, are not due to "feelings of alienation" but to "defective social environments in homes, schools, factories and elsewhere." The result is often violent acts against the society that has failed them.

But, says Skinner, through a technology of behavior, "it should be possible to design a world in which behavior likely to be punished seldom or never occurs." In short, a Utopia is needed, a place where there will be no wars, no quarreling, no overpopulation, minimal pollution, adequate food and shelter for all, and lots of time for art and games. Just because Utopias have not yet worked, he adds, is not certain proof that one never will. The large picture for the future, according to the psychologist, will include behavioral and genetic engineering as a part of the cultural design. "To refuse to control," he says, "is to leave control not to the person himself but to other parts of the social and nonsocial environments. A permissive government is a government that leaves control to other sources. Only when other forms of control are available is that government best which governs least." Once the true causes of behavior in humans have been learned, Skinner believes, it will be possible to construct a happier culture by applying the methods of science to human behavior.

Many questions are raised by Skinner's suggestions. Among them are the two posed earlier: Should we exert control because the techniques are available? The end result may be desirable, but what about the means? We might also wonder whether we like the idea of giving up those inalienable rights of the individual. Think about some of the other questions raised in this book and apply them here. But when you do, remember that in this field of ethics and morals there is room for many opinions. Try to examine each point of view carefully and recognize that there is disagreement before you make a personal judgment. The worst thing you can do is to accept something blindly — especially in the field of medical techniques — as they are proposed or developed. Says Dr. Amitai Etzioni, the eminent sociologist: "Medical technology has improved to the point that it is possible to open a Pandora's box of decisions without any institutional provisions for thinking through responsibility for them. Decisions facing us now are like a genetic steam engine. In the beginning of the Industrial Revolution, technology created the steam engine. Nobody asked what it meant in terms of mass production, industrialization, or urbanization. In genetics, the same is true. The opening wedges are here and they are not hypothetical."

Human experimentation also raises many questions. Consider the celebrated Tuskegee syphilis experiment. The study was begun in 1932 in Tuskegee, Alabama, and was designed to determine the long-term effects of the venereal disease on untreated victims. All of the participants — all black males, 85 percent of whom had less than a sixth-grade education — were persuaded to join a social "lodge" named after the public-health nurse who supervised the study in the field. The experiment was sponsored by the U.S. government, and inducements to join included offers of free medicine (except for syphilis), free rides in government limousines with government decals on the doors, cash payments to each of thirty-five dollars, inexpensive burials, and free hot meals on examination day. Soon the lack of treatment began to have serious repercussions. By 1936 heart disease linked to syphilis had infected many among the group of 399. And by 1944 the mortality rate for the syphilitics was double that of the control group. But worse than all of this, when penicillin became widely available after World War II, none of the victims was treated with it. And although many of the men were in the advanced stages of the disease, they were not informed of the nature of the illness. According to the

NAACP Legal Defense Fund, men who were "accidentally" treated by nonparticipating doctors were dropped from the program. By 1972 there were only seventy-four known survivors, all with various disabilities due to untreated syphilis.

More than a dozen studies of the experiment were published in medical journals, but there were only a few protests. It wasn't until the story was broken by Associated Press reporter Jean Heller, in July of 1972, that a public outcry was raised. Later a number of reports suggested that the study added little to medical knowledge of syphilis. The case raises important questions about informed consent of the subjects and proper guidelines for human experiments. These are questions that must be answered quickly.

Up to this point, we have used the term "engineering" to refer to the manipulation or management of cellular and brain "machinery." The words "engineering," "machinery," and "mechanism" have been figures of speech in this book, although they do convey with relative accuracy what scientists who work in this area are doing, and with what. But there is another form of biological engineering that is more than a metaphor. It is called biomedical engineering, and it is truly an alliance between biologists, physicians, and engineers — the latter group including electrical, chemical, and mechanical engineers. Biomedical engineering's goal is to solve medical problems and to improve bodily function and mobility through the development of devices called prostheses. These are artificial parts — heart valves, limbs, dentures, joints, arteries, eyes, and pumps — made of various metals, plastics, and synthetic fibers. Biomedical engineering has much progressed since the days of the seafarers' peg legs and hooked hands. Today we can talk, and not facetiously, about a *real* Six Million Dollar Man — television's ex-astronaut who possessed atomic-powered legs and a zoom-lens eye. While we have not quite reached that technological level, the implantation of artificial devices in human beings, and the linking of patients to external devices like the artificial-kidney and heart-lung machines, has become a rather routine part of modern medical practice.

Consider this case. In 1976 the National Heart and Lung Institute disclosed that blood pumps had been implanted for the first time in humans. The pumps are known as LVADs (for "left ventricular assist device"), and are implanted in the body and connected by tubing through the skin to a bedside power console. They are not totally implantable artificial hearts and are not, in their current state, designed to be used for more than a few days or weeks — the time required for some failed hearts to heal. With further testing, they may be improved on enough to pave the way for permanent, independent assist pumps, and even artificial hearts that would replace the natural organ.

Large animals have been successfully maintained with the LVAD. And for some time, researchers have felt the device was ready for trial in humans — for when the heart fails to resume its pumping action after open-heart surgery, for instance. Two models of the pump were used in the tests on the four patients. One, with mechanical plastic valves, was set in the abdomen; the other, made with valves taken from pigs, was implanted in the chest. All four patients — who were not otherwise expected to survive, according to the surgeons — died.

All of the doctors involved were reluctant to discuss their work or disclose how long the patients had survived. "As far as I'm concerned," one of the physicians told me, "there is nothing more to say about the research, except that more work is required. And insofar as where exactly the operation was performed, I consider that privileged information between physician and patient's family."

Several issues are raised by this case. Among them is one involving consent information. The patient should know, for instance, that if the device works, he or she may be dependent on it for the remainder of life, and that no one can be sure what the quality of that life will be. The decision to implant such a device will often be too difficult to be made by patient and physician alone, and may require a third party. One wonders who made the decisions in the four cases. Furthermore, since the devices invariably fail after a short time, what alternatives could possibly have been given the patients? A heart transplant, as the American Heart Association's Committee on Ethics puts it, is at present an option of limited quality, while a totally implanted artificial heart is not yet practical. There is the matter of public involvement in such research, particularly where it pays the bill for government-sponsored work. Doesn't the public have a right to know more? Should the public be brought into the decision-making? One of the Heart and Lung Institute officials has indicated that more implants were planned to buy time for dying patients. Given the current state of the art, how much time? And to what purpose?

"When a trial has implications for social support by the general community or has more than routine medical or human interest, investigators should consult widely in the community to inform its members and to share its views and concerns," the American Heart Association committee said, in a recent consideration of the LVAD. "There is an ethical responsibility to plan in advance how best to inform the public reliably while respecting the privacy of the trial participants."

One cannot help but wonder if the Heart and Lung Institute would have been as reticent — or the hospitals as restrained — if the patients had survived for great periods of time.

The issues we have been discussing throughout this book are, as you have seen, extremely complex and sensitive ones. And the easy way out would be to adopt an attitude that says, in effect: let's quit probing where we shouldn't before it's too late; or, let's not ever use human beings in research studies. Such a stance not only goes against the commitment science has made to accumulate new knowledge, a commitment that is at the very heart of all scientific inquiry. It also throws a barrier across the path of researchers who must fulfill science's other great commitment — the betterment of humankind through eradication of disease and by giving all of us a better world in which to live.

This is not to imply that no holds should be barred, that there are no moral rules. No rational person, for instance, would want to emulate the abominable experiments of the Nazis who not only tried to selectively eliminate "defective" humans but also went so far as to kidnap young Nordic girls — blond, tall, and blue-eyed — and force them to mate with carefully screened German soldiers. The object, of course, was to breed a population of "pure" stock that would be part of an empire destined to last for thousands of years.

There must, obviously, be guidelines. But the guidelines must not be so restrictive as to stand in the way of what science, in the last analysis, is — a never-ending quest.

Index